God
in a Bottle

Jamie Richir

ISBN 978-1-64258-006-8 (paperback)
ISBN 978-1-64258-007-5 (digital)
ISBN 978-1-64299-463-6 (hardcover)

Christian Faith Publishing, Inc.
832 Park Avenue
Meadville, PA 16335
www.christianfaithpublishing.com

Printed in the United States of America

July 24, 2015

"I'm sorry, Mrs. Richir, it is cancer." I sat down and a humming started in my ears. I asked the doctor to repeat himself. "I'm sorry, what did you say?" This couldn't be right. Just yesterday, he said it didn't look like anything, but he'd let me know today for sure when the results came back. This can't happen to me. I'm healthy and there is absolutely no breast cancer history on either side of my family. None. There is certainly some mistake. But he wasn't done. "We don't have all the results back yet, but it doesn't look like breast cancer, it looks like something that has metastasized from someplace else." *Boom*, I'm stage 4 terminal cancer. This is all wrong. I started to cry. "We'll let you know as soon as the pathology report comes back, I'm very sorry."

A couple months ago, I'd had some strange feelings in my left breast. It was about time for a mammogram, so I called my GP, Dr. Connor, and asked her to set it up at the local hospital. The mammography machine was new, and the local hospital was pretty proud of it, so I was all set. I went in, told her about what was happening, and she looked really closely at my left breast. Nope, nothing. I was good. Phew! I said a quick thank-you prayer to God and went on my merry way.

Fast forward a couple months and nothing had changed, but I was still having that strange feeling so I called my doctor again. "Can we take another look at this? I just really feel like something has changed and I want to be sure." This time, she scheduled a mammogram on the left side only and a sonogram to follow if nothing was found. During the sonogram, they found a teeny tiny little "nothing" and had time to do a biopsy right then, so I said, "Sure. Let's do this and be done." The doctor said it didn't look like a cancer, but he'd call me tomorrow and let me know for sure. I was thinking it was just some pre-menopausal thing. I was fifty-eight and still having regular periods. Little did I know that was an indicator that put me in a higher risk category for breast cancer.

I never expected this. Never.

I hung up the phone and looked at Keith. He didn't even know I'd gone in for the tests; I was so sure everything was going to be just fine. "I have breast cancer," I told him. I covered my face and wept. This doesn't happen to me. This happens to other people. I am healthy. I don't drink, I don't smoke, and I'm healthy. I couldn't catch my breath. I got up and went to our sun porch and picked up my Bible. I started pleading with God. Oh God, oh God. I couldn't think past that. I was manic and I was paralyzed with fear. I cried and thumbed through my Bible, looking for the magic verse that would tell me that this was all a big mistake that would be corrected and everything was going to be just fine. I couldn't calm down or quit crying or catch my breath. I bowed my head and cried, "Oh, God, please be with me." That's when I felt it; a calm that quieted me. And the verse: "Be still and know that I am God," came to my mind. I felt an amazing peace wash over me and I knew that God had come near. He was holding me in my darkest moment. I was resting in God's peace that passes understanding, and I could calm myself and take a good, close look at this cancer that had entered my life.

He had been with me a couple years ago when my retina detached. I ended up having four eye surgeries for that, but the one that I will always remember was when the doctor went in and removed the vitreous fluid and replaced it with oil. I could see the instruments coming into my eye and I was starting to have a panic attack. I'd never had one, but I was starting to feel panic. My breathing started getting faster and my mind was racing. I was thinking, *God, I can't handle this! I know I'll never get more than you and I can handle together, but I'm thinking you've forgotten what a sissy I am!* The

4

doctor told me the only thing I was able to move was my jaw and no matter what I did, do *not* move it. So I was doing a soft wailing with my mouth closed, trying with all my heart to stave off the panic I felt coming. I was pleading with God to help me. Then I saw it. It was like I was there, in a beautiful field near a creek. I could feel the wind and see it moving the wildflowers. I could hear the water as it traveled over the rocks in the creek bed. Across the creek were deer in the woods, grazing. It was a beautiful place and I felt relaxed and calm. I don't know exactly what happened, but I believe it was God helping me stay calm enough to get through that surgery. I did. He got me through that, and I knew he was already prepared to get me through this trial.

I thought about God and how he knew me and loved me. This cancer didn't change that. He knew it was coming. That one phone call had changed my life, but it hadn't surprised God.

Looking at it now, he had planned out everything I would need. My mom and dad had moved into the apartment we'd built downstairs last summer. My dad was starting to have some health issues, and it was good to have them here so they didn't have to look after the yard and the snowplowing and all that heavy lifting stuff. I never guessed that moving my mom and dad into our home would be more for me than for them. My daughter and son-in-law and sweet granddaughter Zoie had built on the next property over and would be there to help me too. I had a preplanned wait staff all ready to help. God had even provided for this when I'd lost my job a few years back. I had worked for a company where I was just a number and they had a tough sick leave policy. My new job was working for a company that really appreciated me and knew how hard I worked for them. My new job was working for an incredible man, Jim Berlin who knew me and encouraged me and appreciated my determination and work ethics. He had staffed his company with like-minded, hardworking, good people. I loved going to work each day and I knew he would do whatever he could to work with me through this. All of this was planned by an amazing God who knew ahead of time what I was going to need. I didn't know that at the time, but looking back, it all fits so perfectly into place.

Right now, I knew that I had cancer, possibly stage 4 cancer, and I needed to think about what needed to be done. That night, I traveled down all those dead-end roads where I died and thought about what I had already prepared for, and what still needed to be done. I thought about Keith who had been disabled for the past twenty-eight years and needed me to provide health insurance for him. He also needed me to make any phone calls because he was almost deaf and had difficulty communicating; I was his interpreter to the outside world. How would he survive without me?

I thought about Marcie, my amazing daughter. She had been such a gift from God and was my dearest and sweetest friend now that she was a grown up. Had I left anything undone for her? She might not really need me anymore, but I was a big part of her life, and I sure wanted to be here for her. To do anything I could do to help make her life easier. I sure needed her! And sweet Zoie, my six-year-old granddaughter; I really wanted to be a part of her life. She was the joy in my life and I wanted to see her grow up.

Then there was my sweet mom and dad living in my basement apartment . . . how would that work if I died? How was all this going to work, God? I needed to live. I had to live.

But I knew that whatever the outcome, God had me and he also had those people I loved, and he would take care of them after I was gone. He was in control, and if I died, they would all be okay. But that night, he gave me a verse, Jeremiah 29:5, "I know the thoughts that I think toward you, says the Lord, thoughts of peace and not of evil, to give you a future and a hope." I knew I was going to live. God gave me hope and a future. I just didn't know then what a difficult journey I was going on. I only knew that God was going to be with me, and he'd prepared the path and lined it with people who loved me, along with wonderful prayer warriors to see me through.

So for today, my prayer was, "Please, God, let this be breast cancer." Crazy, huh?

My mind was racing with the question of what kind of cancer this could be if it wasn't primarily breast cancer. Please, God, let it be just breast cancer. The irony of that "just breast cancer" wasn't lost on me. My thoughts went to the things lately that I'd been forgetting. Did I have brain cancer? Oh my goodness! I don't want to lose my faculties and die a horrible death where my family has to see me quickly or, even worse, slowly deteriorate while I blow through any money I have set aside for Keith to live on after I'm gone. Please don't let me die before Zoie will remember how much I loved her. So many things I was asking God for, begging God for. I was worrying. Didn't God say something about worry? Yes, he said not to worry. It was crazy to worry about what was wrong. I didn't even know yet and I wouldn't find out until Monday. I was only guessing at what I was dealing with. In the meantime, God was holding me. I was in good hands.

Word of cancer travels at the speed of lightning. While my mind was spinning with so many questions, the word of my cancer started to travel through my friends and family. Calls started coming in from people concerned for me. Keith fielded those calls because I wasn't ready to talk about it yet. I'm a crier by nature. I cry at Hallmark movies, parades, and anything the least bit emotional, and this put me way over the top. We had been blessed with wonderful, lifelong friends, Den and Val. They were two of our closest friends. They came to see me and let both of us know that they were here for anything we needed. I cried, of course. But they loved us and I felt so blessed to have such wonderful friends. They would come all throughout my journey. I couldn't seem to talk without crying. If they were saying something sweet, I cried. If it was funny, I cried. I was so incredibly emotional. But it was what it was and everyone got used to me. It wasn't that I was so sad, I was just so overwhelmed with emotions and that was the way it manifested itself in me. Some people shut down, I cry. I was also so tired. This whole thing had been draining. My girlfriend Coleen, who is also a prayer warrior, called and said to listen to Jason Crabb's song, *Through the Fire*. Oh my goodness, talk about crying! But it was a beautiful song and it gave me hope, reminding me that God would hold me through this fire. One of my favorite calls was from my brother-in-law, Mike, who said he was waiting for word so he could pray, "Thank you, Jesus, for the scare." I loved that optimism. I needed that hope. For now, my family was gathering around and trying to distract me, and my friends were praying for me. I'd asked that they pray that this be "just breast cancer." That was the prayer for the weekend. Monday, we would find out. I truly felt blessed to have people. That is no small thing.

But the hospital didn't call on Monday. I was thinking, *Okay, no news is good news, right?*

Dr. Connor sent me for a cancer marker blood test. This would show how long the cancer had been in my blood. I believe it showed how aggressive the cancer is and something about positives and negatives. It would help the doctors decide what kind of treatment I needed. Maybe I'd get lucky and just need a lumpectomy and a little radiation and that'd be it.

No call on Tuesday, either, so I called them when I got back to my office. Yes, the pathology report is back: it *is* breast cancer. My first answered prayer. Thank you, God!

I made a list of people that included my family, church, friends, and the people I worked with and called on. I'm an outside sales person for a logistics company, and many of the people I call on are Christians. I sent emails to all those people with my prayer request. I knew these people would actually pray and it was so comforting to know that. I had one of my customers, Julie, send me a text with a picture of a car in a restaurant parking lot. She and her daughter had gone to Erie to have lunch. They parked next to a car that had "Pray for Jamie" written on the back window. What an amazing God! He knows exactly what I need. That was such an incredible encouragement to me. Of course, I cried.

I felt so blessed after she sent this to me. I am
being held up by my prayer warriors.

The first email I sent out asking for prayer was

> I have a praise and a prayer request.
>
> Today, we are celebrating an answered
> prayer. I got word on Friday afternoon that I
> have breast cancer. They didn't think it was actu-
> ally breast cancer, but another cancer that had
> metastasized and moved to the breast. I've been
> waiting for the pathology reports to come back to
> see what it was.
>
> Today, we got word that it is in fact breast
> cancer, and we are rejoicing and giving God the

glory for the first of many answered prayers and miracles he has in store for me. It is amazing to see how he has worked this out in a way that I am thankful to "only have breast cancer," . . . who says that?

I can see already how he has gone before me into this fire and is leading the way. I am looking forward to see what other prayers he will answer and see how I can be used by Him to show the HOPE we have in Christ. I won't say I'm excited about the fight I'm about to enter, but I am looking forward to seeing His hand guiding my way. I understand the calm he brings to a troubled soul now. What an amazing God we serve.

I've already had several opportunities to testify of what a powerful, loving, prayer answering God I serve. How fun!!

Please praise God for the wonderful news today. I am selfish enough to pray that I can have a lumpectomy and not a mastectomy, so that is my current prayer. Pray also that I will keep in the forefront of my mind that I am a living testimony to God's power and love. That God will give me strength to battle this with that goal in mind. And pray for my family. This has been very hard on them too.

Dr. Connor had also scheduled an appointment for today with a surgeon she had confidence in. He would have the results of my biopsy test. I was still hopeful this was going to be a mistake. I still felt that this kind of thing didn't happen to me. I was going into the surgeon's office, and he was going to look everything over and say I could go home, there'd been a mistake—I was fine.

I go in, strip to the waist, and meet the surgeon with a paper half-top on. I know this is nothing, but the stupid paper top barely closed at the top, and I just felt naked and afraid. He came in, introduced himself, looked at my chest, and sat at his little desk, looking over my test results. He explained that it was breast cancer and some of the test results were good and some were troubling. It was estrogen positive and that was good. On the other hand, they like the cancer growth rate to be around 2 or 3 and mine was 25. That was very troubling because it was growing very quickly. I needed an MRI to see if it had gone beyond the breast and into the lymph nodes. I would probably need a mastectomy, but with this rate of aggression, he'd recommend chemotherapy first. "But let's get the MRI and talk again when we have all the facts." After the MRI, he would know what to do. While I was in the office, he did a punch biopsy of the skin because he had a suspicion that it had already involved the skin. He asked me if I had any questions. I had so many questions, I didn't know where to start, so the only question I asked was, "Can I live through this?" His answer was vague, but somewhat positive, so I latched on to that. My ears started that humming again. "I've been thinking a lot about this since the biopsy, and I believe that God is going to heal me," I said. "Are you a Christian?" He paused before answering me. "I had a woman come in here a couple of years ago and she said God was going to heal her. She didn't take any treatment and she died. I don't think I pray as much as I should and I haven't been to church in a while."

"I didn't say God wasn't going to use doctors, surgeons, medicine, and treatments to heal me, but he's the one that's going to heal me. You watch and see what amazing things God is going to do through me." The nurse said "Amen" and smiled at me. We set up the port surgery before I left, and they would call me for the MRI appointment. I was going to rely on God to get me through this, and I was going to be sure to have doctors that knew God and listened to him.

> Hi,
>
> Thank you for the prayers. I met with the surgeon for the first time. He did a skin biopsy at the office and I have an MRI scheduled. When we get the results of these two tests, he'll know how to proceed.

There were some things on the pathology report he liked and some he didn't, and the fact that he felt a need to do a biopsy was part of the bad news, so please keep praying.

I still have a huge battle ahead, but knowing you are praying for me means the world. I asked him if it turns out to be the worst case scenario, can I live through this and his answer was yes. So I'm going with that.

God has walked in front of me through this fire so far and he's promised never to leave me or forsake me. AND he's given me such a wonderful support team. Thank you for being there and for praying. I can't say enough how much that means to me. I believe in the power of prayer. Thank you for it.

Today with the news that it was primary breast origin was like winning the lottery, so today is a great day!! Jamie

Dr. Connor called me that evening and said the cancer marker test had come back negative and that was great news. This was a brand-new cancer. She said we were going to get through this. I was so thankful for her call. It meant a lot to me to hear my doctor say that. I trusted her. She had always been completely honest with me; sometimes brutally honest, but I respected that. My hope was in God, but I was also finding I craved positive comments. This was a new need I had. I was so grateful to her for taking the time to call me that night at home.

Her encouraging words mattered to me. I had gone down all those roads where the bad stuff happened, and now I was going to concentrate on everything positive and not allow those negative thoughts into my mind. I was going to live and God was my healer. I wasn't interested in hearing anything else.

I was still thanking God that it was breast cancer, and for the good cancer marker test and for all the people he'd put in my life; my beautiful family and such wonderful friends. I was so blessed. God was carrying me through this right now, and I felt so blessed to know that so many people were lifting my name up to God for healing.

Even though I knew God had me and people were praying for me and I wasn't supposed to worry, I still had trouble turning my mind off enough to sleep at night. I'd go over and over what was happening and think about what could or would happen. It had been a couple of nights and I wasn't sleeping much at all. I knew that couldn't go on. He reminded me through my Bible reading that he would never leave me or forsake me, so I started counting my blessings when I lay down. I started thanking God for all the beautiful things he'd done for me throughout my life, and now through this mess. That peace I felt the first day was no small thing, and I still got an amazing boost just thinking about it. I was thanking him for loving me enough to be here with me through this and surrounding me with wonderful people. I prayed he would help me turn this trial into a testimony. I prayed my words and actions as I navigated this new challenge would be a testimony to the hope I had through Jesus. When I started to talk to God as I lay down to sleep, I started sleeping like a baby.

Keith, on the other hand, was still having a difficult time sleeping. He had been a rock for me and he was having a difficult time turning his mind off too. I almost think it's harder to watch someone you love go through this than go through it yourself.

I'd known I had breast cancer for a week now. I was choosing to completely rely on God to get me through this. Even though I occasionally grabbed it back and worried over it, I was doing that less and less. I was settling into the facts. I had breast cancer, I might need a mastectomy, but first chemotherapy. My cancer was growing quickly, and I was actually starting to feel a lump under my left arm. That was new. I wondered if it was because we woke the sleeping beast with the biopsy or if this would have happened regardless.

I was sleeping fine and Keith was finally starting to sleep too. It's amazing what you can deal with when you take it one breath at a time, and when you have faith in an amazing, loving, prayer-answering God. I felt "safe" now. Sounds silly, but I did. God is in control. I've accepted that I'm going to have to go through a lot of new, painful things, but I'm not going alone. Not only was God here with me, but He'd given me so many beautiful, praying people. I felt an overwhelming love from God and from my family and friends. Life is precious. Each day is precious. I think I knew that before, but I never had to live like I might be dying. Now each minute had value. I had already changed some of my thoughts and priorities. I seemed to have more patience. How strange was that? I may be running out of time, but I seemed to be more patient. Nothing seems to rattle me anymore. I guess when you aren't sure if you'll make it to Christmas, you don't want to waste time looking too deeply into the little things. And I guess by little things, I now mean things that aren't going to kill me today.

Sweet friends had come and brought dinner. Some had taken us out to dinner. I was being intentional about spending more time with my family. My mom, Marcie, and Zoie had spent an afternoon doing our fingernails and toes just to have fun together.

One of my friends, Dawn, had gone through this about a year before. I had prayed with her and kept close tabs on her because she was having such a hard time accepting everything she was going through. She was right there for me now. She'd been through chemotherapy and a mastectomy and had just gotten her hair back that summer. She was here, doing well, feeling good. She was such an encourager. I appreciated her calls and positive comments.

We were having a long stretch of beautiful sunny days, and I was enjoying every bit of sunshine I could. I'd park a little farther from the doors when I made my calls so I could take little walks. I'd run in and change my clothes and come right back outside after work. I felt closer to God outside in the sunshine. I was scheduled for surgery to get a port in and an MRI scan. Once those were done, we'd get busy fighting this cancer. Until then, I was going to enjoy these beautiful days God was giving me.

I'd made a joint call with the head of our international department, Abi. She is a beautiful, intelligent young gal and she is a Christian. We had lots of time to talk on the way down, and she said she had prayed and declared my healing and it was done—just a matter of time now. I was so blessed by that. I had also asked God to heal me in Christ's name, and I believed it to be so. But hearing that others were also asking for that was such a sweet blessing. It's amazing how much I needed to hear positive things about this fight I was heading into. I'm going to remember that if I ever have a friend or family member in the fight for their life with cancer, or anything else that threatens their life. If I need it, I'm guessing it's a pretty normal thing and everyone needs it.

My MRI scan was for 7:00 a.m. in Olean. It's about an hour from home, but it's in my sales territory, and they had one of the newest machines around, so we opted for Olean. I'd have my scan and then make sales calls in the Olean area. I kept telling myself I was not nervous. This was just a test to get more knowledge to know how to best fight this cancer.

Coleen had texted me very early that morning, saying that she was praying for me. Coleen would become a rock I rely on through this journey. She was always there with a Bible verse or a word of encouragement or a page from her daily devotions. I needed her. And, not least of all, she cleaned my house for me! She had lost her job a couple years back, and I don't remember if she asked me or if I asked her, but she ended up cleaning my house every other week for me. She said she loved cleaning. I truly find that hard to believe because to me, cleaning the house is many hours wasted, but necessary so you don't live in squalor. She helped me keep my house clean and I paid her to do it. Although as far as I'm concerned, I could never pay her enough to do what she did for me.

Joy called me on the way down. Joy and I had been friends since junior high school. She was such an amazing prayer warrior for me too. We had been friends since we were kids, and even though she'd moved to Florida and raised her family, we'd remained close all those years, and I loved her. I needed her.

I had come to know Brenda and Mike from a darling little store I visited frequently; too frequently, if truth be told, but I had fallen in love with this couple. They had such a sweet spirit and I just loved their little store. I loved all the country things they built and sold, but I also loved them and the music and the smell of the lovely wax melts they burned in the store. Just everything about that store drew me in, and once I met those two, I was hooked. Brenda and Mike were both devout Christians, and we'd started praying for each other. Paula who works with them said it's a "thin space". She says it's close to heaven and I agree.

I sent an email to my prayer warriors that morning:

> I'm getting ready to head out for my MRI. I'm having it in Olean. I could have had it in Buffalo, but this way I can make calls afterwards and it's a nicer drive. Today is my last test and then Thursday I find out what the results are.
>
> It's either going to be massive chemo and radiation before I can have probably double mastectomy surgery. Or surgery, testing while they're in there and then whatever follow-up they (and Roswell who is consulting on the treatment) feel is necessary. Obviously I'm hoping and praying for the easier road. I won't know until Thursday.
>
> The reason for the huge difference in the two treatments is because the doctor said there was a possibility the cancer had spread to my breast skin and that is a very aggressive cancer. He did a biopsy in the office when I was there last. But honestly, God is in control and he's got it all mapped out for me. It's so obvious from all the test schedules, the timing of everything and just the prayers He's answered already that He's got me.
>
> Everyone I've asked to pray is praying and I really want them to see the hope and the calm God gives His people through the fires of life. That's also my prayer. I will have a testimony that will glorify God through this AND that I'll live!!
>
> Thank you so much for your prayers. God is answering them and keeping me calm and going

ahead of me and paving the way. Let's hope for the best case scenario for Thursday and I'll say "Thank you God for the scare!"

I had some pretty fierce prayer warriors! There's no better feeling than *knowing* someone is really lifting you up to God in prayer. It's such a comfort. I knew my family was praying. They were so faithful to bring my needs to God on my behalf.

I felt those prayers during that test. The nurses were so sweet. Everyone had a story about cancer. They had survived this cancer or someone they knew had that cancer, and they were just fine now. Cancer was absolutely everywhere!

It took a bit of time, it was very loud, and you had to be very still. I found it humorous that I had to lie on my stomach and strategically place the "girls" into square holes. I wondered why they didn't make them round? Must be a guy designed this machine. Silly things that go through your mind at stressful times. It actually made me giggle.

I met again with the surgeon for the results of that MRI and the biopsy he'd done in his office during my last visit.

Again, I stripped down to my waist and put on the little paper half shirt. Ugh. He said the cancer had spread into the centinal node, but didn't look like it had gone up any lymph nodes yet, and it was no place else. My second answered prayer. The punch biopsy he'd taken during my last appointment was clean. A bonus answered prayer! I was starting to feel hopeful. Then he continues, "What we were looking at is a mastectomy and removing the centinal node and any lymph nodes that are affected at that time." But my cancer was too aggressive to operate on first. "You will need chemotherapy, then surgery, then possibly radiation." He gave me the name of the oncologist before I left.

Did I have any questions? What, like how could this be happening to me? Is this real? I needed a mastectomy. I just wanted to get out of there, but first, I wanted to be sure I needed a mastectomy. So I asked, "Why not a lumpectomy?" He told me I actually had two tumors; one in the upper left quadrant and a smaller one in the lower left quadrant. He needed to remove too much to save it. I think he actually said, "Breast conservation is not possible." The aggressive nature of my cancer made these measures necessary, so we didn't want to take any chances it would return. They are going to cut off my breast. I'm having a mastectomy. I'm having a mastectomy. I feel like I'm living on the edge of a nightmare. This can't be happening to me.

I got my referral appointment to the oncologist before I left. The receptionist was so kind. I could see the sympathy in her eyes. *Poor thing,* she must be thinking. Poor thing needs a mastectomy. I really do have cancer.

Keith had driven me to the appointment but waited in the waiting room. I walked to him, looked at him, and turned to walk out to the car. He followed. Once we got into the car, I looked at him and cried. I need a mastectomy, but first, I need to have chemotherapy. My cancer is very aggressive. More crying. Deep breath. Remember that God is in control and he's got me. Somehow, until this point, I'd been hoping that it was going to be a mistake or just a small thing. It wasn't. My reality was that I had aggressive breast cancer that has metastasized to the centinal node, and I needed a mastectomy.

> To my sweet praying friends and family . . .
>
> I didn't get the easy news today I was hoping for but there was some good news in there.
>
> The punch biopsy the doctor took showed negative for cancer that had come through my skin. That was a huge answered prayer, so thank you all for praying. But after looking at the MRI the doctor felt it would be much safer to do 3 months of chemo before I have surgery since I have so many tumors in my breast.
>
> So next week I get a port and the following week I start chemo. When he feels the cancer has shrunk enough to be safe to operate, I will have the surgery. I'm not praying to God today saying, "Thank you for the scare, Lord," like I'd

hoped, but I am saying thank you for that peace that passes understanding. And I will be thanking him from now till the new year for all my praying friends and family who are lifting me up to God for strength and comfort and especially for healing. Thank you so much for your prayers. I can't stress how much they comfort me and will help heal me. God is good and He is in control. He has promised never to leave me or forsake me.

Keep praying and you can be a part of my journey to the other end where I'll say, "Thank you Lord for the healing."

I told the doctor that I had to do the funky chicken at Zoie's wedding so I needed about 25 years yet.

I love you all for keeping me in your thoughts and especially in your prayers. Thank you.

Pray for Keith too. This is really hard on him too.

I've known I have cancer now for two weeks. It seems like a lifetime. I've been running from one test to the next and from one doctor to another with blood work in between. My next stop was to meet with an oncologist; Dr. Ibabao. I waited for quite some time to meet the doctor. I knew he was very busy when I entered his waiting room. It was filled with bald men and women. Some really skinny and some bloated and heavy from whatever treatment they were receiving. As I entered into the rooms past the waiting room, they, too, were filled with people hooked up to poles with several bags hanging from them. Some were sleeping, some were watching TV. Some had people in their rooms and were talking. It was a busy place. Lots of sick people hoping to get well. The whole place was really scary to me today. Maybe I'd get used to it, but right now, it was scary.

Strip down to the waist, but this time, I got to put on a cloth shirt that completely covered me and crossed over, and I felt better sitting there, waiting. Funny how such little things matter.

I met with the nurse practitioner first, and she told me not to eat soy. My cancer was estrogen positive, and soy was recognized by the body as estrogen. I told her that was no problem, I never ate soy. She laughed. I was thinking of soy sauce. What else was soy in? I didn't know it then, but she told me to go home and check my cupboards and refrigerator for soy. She said I'd probably be giving most of my food away and would be shopping for things to replace them.

Dr. Ibabao is a cancer doctor for chemotherapy. He is a beautiful man from the Philippines and he's a Christian. He went over my records and told me what I had. As he was talking about my cancer, he kept shaking his head and saying to himself, "This is bad," and "This is not good." He wasn't really talking to me when he said that, but he was looking at my records and talking to himself. I told him I didn't want to know anything more than what was expected of me and what I could expect from the treatments. He said I would be getting very strong chemotherapy and hopefully it would work. But . . . some cancers do not react to chemotherapy. I wouldn't be getting just three treatments, but five months of it. This increase was necessary. I now had a lump the size of an orange in my left breast. It was growing fast.

I asked him if he was a Christian man and if he believed in miracles. He said yes. He would not be able to do this job if it were not for the miracles he'd witnessed. He believed with his whole heart in God and miracles. I told him the same thing I told the surgeon, "You watch and see what amazing things God is going to do through me and this cancer."

I felt getting Dr. Ibabao was an answered prayer. If everyone was praying for me, God would be able to work through Dr. Ibabao, who would be listening. I felt a bit calmer after this appointment. I need to get the port in, and they would start two weeks after that. He gave me some papers to read and a folder with all kinds of information in it about the chemotherapy I'd be getting, and how to handle the different reactions I might encounter. He scheduled a MUGA scan to be sure my heart was strong enough to take this treatment, and a pet scan to see exactly where the cancer was. It was more detailed than the CAT scan, I guess.

I brought all my paperwork home and decided to check my pantry to see if I did have some soy in my daily diet. I was absolutely shocked at how much. Everything in my cupboard had soy in it. Everything from my peanut better to my oil, my pasta and spaghetti sauce had soy as one of the first couple ingredients. All my salad dressings and even bread had soy. Oh my goodness! Boy, was she right! It took me and Keith, and later my mom and Marcie, lots of trips to the grocery store to find alternatives to my soy-ridden foods.

I checked into outpatient at the local hospital for the port surgery. They would be placing something under my skin that ran into some main artery so they could give me intense chemotherapy and not worry as much about it collapsing my veins from the toxic chemicals I'd be getting. Yikes! I had figured out something about myself. I didn't want to know all the gory details about what was wrong with me and exactly what they were going to do. I just wanted to know what was expected of me, what I could expect from my body from the procedure, and that was about it. My friends were telling me to go online and find out all I could about what kind of cancer I had, and learn everything I could about what to do to help myself. I couldn't. Maybe it's because I'm a coward, maybe I'm not smart enough to understand everything. It didn't matter, I just couldn't do it. I didn't want to know. I explained that to the surgeon when he was trying to educate me. I never intended to be a surgeon or a doctor or even a cancer specialist. I just wanted to be a survivor. I was trusting God to bring me to the right people, and then I was trusting those people to do everything they could to help me live.

This surgery was very emotional for me. I had cancer. No turning back to the time when I was healthy and hadn't heard the word *cancer*. This was real. It was a little surgery and the risk was very minimal, but it was the beginning of a journey I didn't want to go on. It was the start of something I never wanted to deal with. But it was my reality and I needed to get my attitude straight. This was the beginning of when I kicked cancer's butt—with God's help of course. But right now, I was scared. I cried when the nurse came to ask me what I was there for. She brought me a box of Kleenex. I really tried to be strong, but I was scared, really scared. Keith was there with me, but what do you say to someone who's trying unsuccessfully to be brave? He said it was going to be all right, and I knew it would. But for right now, I was scared. I just wanted to wake up and have this all go away.

The surgery was quick and they did an x-ray to be sure everything was placed correctly, and I was released. It had begun. In my mind, the war had begun, and I was going to be victorious. One way or the other; I would win.

> I just got back from getting my A port in. I am scheduled for 4 months of intense chemo and then a mastectomy reconstruction. I get started on the chemo next week so I'm feeling like at least I'm ready to fight now. I have a couple more tests—muga to see if my heart is strong enough for the intense chemo they'll be giving me (which I'm sure it is) and a pet scan to see if it's traveled anyplace else. (Say a prayer)
>
> God has been with me this whole journey and I feel so blessed to have people lifting me up to Him in prayer.
>
> He had given me the peace that passes understanding and I know He'll get me through this.
>
> I just hope they cure this lousy disease before you younger gals have to even worry about it. Hopefully we're really close.
>
> Thank you so much for your thoughts and prayers,
>
> —Jamie

Dawn called me and we talked about the PET scan and the chemotherapy. It looked like I'd be taking the same chemo that she did. The second half of my treatments would change to what they had nicknamed "the red devil." Nice. Dawn said I would definitely lose my hair, probably about the third week in. She had a wig I could wear because she got it but never wore it. She couldn't stand it, so she just wore hats. Wow. I was going to lose my hair, and then they were going to cut off my breast. Maybe both. Wow. How do you process that? I said I was never a vain person, but I guess I actually am. The thought of both of those seemed like a nightmare. Could this really be happening to me? Thank you, God, for this calm you are giving me. I honestly think I'd go mad if I didn't have you holding me. But I do and you are. So now I just keep moving forward, taking each day as it comes, not worrying about tomorrow. I can do this, God, with your help. Help me.

My sweet artist friend Corie came to visit me that week. She is amazing and was so positive and encouraging. I really enjoyed our visit. That need for positive words again. I'm learning so many new things about myself. I gain courage from God and his word and also from people who give me encouragement. I never needed that before, but I sure do now. Dear friends Tom and Julie stopped by. Julie had cross stitched a picture for me with the saying "to a friend's house the way is never long". It was beautiful. She put it in an antique frame that needed new glass. When she brought it to be replaced, Brian, another life long friend who owned the hardware store replaced it and told her to let me know he was thinking of me. That's what living in a small town is. A feeling of community. Having friends you grew up with who love you. I felt loved by everyone involved. Of course I cried.

I had been fervently praying for healing, and I think in the back of my mind, I was thinking that healing would come before too much trouble on my part. As I'd been doing my daily Bible readings and prayers and getting so many beautiful and encouraging verses from God, I'd started praying that his will be done. I was starting to accept that his will was not going to be a quick little procedure or instant healing. I know he can do that, but that wasn't going to be my path. I have my port in, and we are two weeks away from chemo.

We told my granddaughter, Zoie, that I was going to go through some treatments that were going to make me lose my hair. We didn't tell her I had cancer because a little girl had just died from cancer. The surrounding communities had been very involved in supporting this little gal, but she had died just recently, and we didn't want to scare Zoie. She brought me over her dance ponytail. It was a hair piece she wore for her dance recitals. Marcie put her hair up in a ponytail and bobby pinned on this hair piece to make it look like she had long, curly hair. How sweet.

I wrote in my journal on Tuesday 8/18: Today, I believe God is going to heal me. I prayed for it in Christ's name, believe it and know it's going to happen. I'm throwing my whole heart into experiencing God's miracle for me with fresh faith. Giving thanks always to my awesome God."

Tomorrow I have the PET scan. I am really nervous about this test. I do have faith that God has me and will be with me, I just don't know what I am being called to go through and it scares me. I need to just lean into God and let him get me through this. I keep telling myself that everyone is praying for me and God knows what I'm going through and He loves me, but I'm still afraid. I don't want to do any of this, I want to wake up and find out this was all a horrible nightmare. But it's not a nightmare it's real and I have to just trust that God has me. Everyone is saying I'm so strong. I keep telling them that I'm not strong. I was a puddle on the floor when I found out I had cancer. It wasn't until I really turned to God and literally cried out to Him that I got strength—enough strength to get though each day and enough strength to get through this next test.

I sent another email asking for prayer.

> Hi
>
> I was hoping I could get each one of you to pay for my pet scan tomorrow at 11.
>
> I know God is going to heal me even if it's spread, but it would be such an encouragement if the cancer was only in the breast. So I'm praying for that. Please pray with me. I'll let you all know asap I do what the results are.
>
> Thanks so much!!
>
> —Jamie

I had accidentally typed *pay* not *pray*. One of my customers sent back an email, saying he'd gladly pray for me, but he wasn't going to send money and put a smiley face after it. Oh my goodness! I was mortified! I sent another email, saying, "Oh my goodness, I was asking for prayer, not payment." Everyone laughed. It was a good way to lighten up the mood. I was still a little embarrassed, but everyone else was entertained. It's good to be humble. I felt those prayers calm me. I felt safe and protected. No longer scared.

Keith and I stopped at Brenda and Mike's store after the scan. Mike said a beautiful prayer for me and Keith.

The next day, my journal had 2 Kings 20:5: "I have heard your prayers I have seen your tears; surely I will heal you." Not a coincidence.

I got a beautiful card from one of my customers, Audrey, saying that she'd prayed for the healing that God was already going to give me. I love those positive notes and calls. It was exactly what I needed today to remind me that God was there and he had me.

I got so many beautiful, encouraging cards. Tony and Mindy sent one every week. I was so touched by their love and thoughtfulness. Donna and Bill sent cards often and even popped in a lottery ticket now and again. How fun! I really enjoyed that—made me smile. Barb, one of my sweet customers sent a picture of an adorable baby girl dressed up like a little football player that told me to be strong and keep fighting. I put that up on my desk. It made me smile every time I looked at it. Jessica sent me flowers and a card that said I was going to be fine. I loved that! Kathy sent me a beautiful little box filled with positive thoughts printed on individual cards. I was encouraged by every single one of those as I opened them each day. Cindy, another dear customer sent me daily pictures of her vacation and all the beautiful things she did and saw. Steve and Shari sent me a wonderful blanket embroidered with a heart and a beautiful get well message – so thoughtful. Ronda stopped by on her way home from picking up her new little puppy. I got her meet Gemma on her first day with her new mom. It was wonderful! All of these gestures meant so much to me. I would have never thought to do these things before I got sick. Before I knew how much those little loving gestures meant. I felt surrounded by people who were so thoughtful and loving and encouraging. I was blessed by each of these acts of kindness, blessed by my friends and family and blessed by God. I was blessed.

I didn't hear the results from the PET scan before the weekend. We had a lot of company that weekend. Everyone wanted to come and tell me they were praying for me, and thinking of me, and to please let them know if they can do anything. I felt so surrounded by love from my friends and my family and my God. I am blessed.

I had the MUGA scan on Monday. Still no word of the PET scan yet. I didn't get the results of all of the tests until my appointment with the surgeon on Thursday. I had the appointment with the surgeon on Thursday. The cancer had not spread beyond the breast.

Now *this* was amazing answered prayer. To God be the glory! God is my strong anchor. I was okay. We were flying high on that news and would get through the weekend on a wonderful euphoric high . . . we thought.

> Today I am celebrating God's incredible love for me and thanking him for the answered prayer I got at the doctor's office this afternoon. One of my most recent and urgent prayers was that the cancer had not spread yet. **Today I found out that it has not.** Praise God! Even my doctor was surprised at this news. I asked him to keep praying for me so he could be part of the miracle God has already given me .
>
> I am so blessed to have all of you praying for me. I can't tell you how much it strengthens me and lifts me up. You are all a part of this wonderful answered prayer from a loving and very present Heavenly Father. When I went through the Pet scan I felt happy and safe. That could only be your prayers and God's love because I was afraid of that test and what it was going to show. That was when I had to just leave it at God's feet and allow him to get me through it. He has, and I am joyful and thankful and so humbled and blessed all at the same time. What an amazing God we serve!!
>
> Celebrate with me today, thanking God for this answered prayer. He is a prayer answerer and a miracle worker still for those who belong to Him. Thank you for being his arms around me and surrounding me with your prayers and love.
>
> I start chemotherapy tomorrow or Monday for the next five months. Please keep praying for me and I'll keep you updated as God answers our prayers for me to be cancer free at the end of this

journey. Please keep Keith and my family in your prayers too. This has been an incredible roller coaster ride for all of us.

Prayer is so powerful.

—Jamie

I had prayed that the doctors would have wisdom on how to treat me. I was trusting that this was the time it took to get the best treatment planned. I just wanted to either be healed or get started. This waiting was really hard. I think the not knowing what's happening was the hardest. My daughter would later ask me what the hardest part of the journey was, and after some thought, I told her hearing the news the first time. That call on Friday, saying, "I'm sorry, Mrs. Richir, it is cancer," was the hardest part, I think. But the waiting wasn't easy!

Coleen called me and said that God has told her that he is already healing me. I believe it. I just don't know what he has in store for me yet. Ultimately, I believe I will be healed.

Friday morning, I had an appointment with an organization called Lilly's Hope. They help ladies feel beautiful through their chemotherapy treatments by giving them wigs. I knew I'd lose my hair, and this seemed like a better alternative to me than just wearing hats all the time. I was still hopeful I would be able to make sales calls through some of my treatments, and this would help me continue to look professional. I got a cute wig after trying on about ten. The lady was just the sweetest gal. She had not been through cancer, but knew many family members and friends who had, so she did this as a volunteer service for those of us who needed it. It was sponsored through the Zonta's club in town. I'd never given something like this a thought, and now here I was getting treated like a queen by people I didn't even know. What a beautiful thing to do for ladies trying to cope with a cancer/chemo diagnosis. It was going to be a great weekend. Both the good report on the cancer yesterday and my new wig. I was feeling happy. Held. Able to cope.

I was on my way home Friday afternoon and had just pulled into the local grocery store parking lot. I was going to stop and grab something for dinner. Marcie called me, "Mom, where are you?" I told her and she said, "Maybe you better get right home. Dad just called Mike on his cell phone. He's up on the hill and he's had a tractor accident. Mike is on his way up with a chain saw to help." I drove right through the parking lot toward home. It was just a couple minutes away. About halfway, I got a call from Keith. His breathing was really labored, and he asked where I was. "On my way home, Keith. Marcie said you'd had an accident. Are you okay?" "No. I'm pinned under the tractor and we can't get the tree off me. Come quick, I'm in trouble." I hung up the phone and called 911. What was I going to do with him pinned under the tractor? I told them my husband was pinned under a tractor and where he was and to hurry. Fast. I called Norm next. Norm and Brenda are wonderful friends that live a couple miles away. They are neighbors in a country kind of way. Norm is a farmer and I knew he'd probably be on a tractor in one of his fields – it was summertime. He answered and I told him what was happening and asked him to come quickly to see if he could help.

I drove right through the cornfield to get to Keith. When I got there, Keith was stuck on the tractor and a huge tree limb was pushing him forward up under the front of the tractor. Michael was trying to start the stupid chainsaw but having no luck. Keith was pasty and in pain, sweating like crazy. I asked Michael to come around my side of the tractor, and maybe between the two of us, we could move the limb enough to get Keith free.

Somehow, miraculously, it worked. I was even able to hold it for a minute while Michael got his shoulder under Keith's hip to help lift him up and out of the tractor. He got down from the tractor and leaned on the side, and that's when everyone started showing up.

"Did you call 911?"

"Yep, of course I did. How was I going to help get you out from underneath a tractor?"

"I didn't say under, I said IN! Call them back and stop it!"

Too late. Norm had called a closer neighbor, Brian, to come with a tractor. All the rescue people started showing up, and the police and fire trucks all piled in. We probably had about forty or fifty rescue people there to help Keith. We had everything from police trucks to heavy-duty tow trucks they'd brought to get the tractor off Keith. I felt so overwhelmed that so many people were here to help save my husband. We are in a rural area, and every one of those people, aside from the police, were volunteering their time. There is so much good in the world! Keith was fine after a trip to the emergency room to check his new hip. But I learned that we were not alone in our struggles. People were there to help. We just needed to ask. But I did tell Keith I couldn't handle all that drama right now, and he needed to behave! If he's off to do something that he thinks he'd better bring his phone for in case he gets into trouble, then he better not do it! For now. So much for the calm, relaxing weekend! But Keith was okay and I was calming down. Life was good and God was in control. I had learned a valuable lesson. People love to help. You just need to ask them to.

We'd been very independent and felt pride in the fact that we'd been able to make it on our own without any help. We'd been blessed to be the helpers up until now. I realized that had been a blessing to be thankful for, not a source of pride. I was learning all sorts of new things already. I almost couldn't wait to see what God was going to do with me on this journey I was embarking on. I didn't know what was coming, but I did know he would carry me through it if I needed it. And I also knew that he had given me so many wonderful friends and such a supportive, beautiful family. I was going to be fine. I already had so much to be thankful for.

"Does your need seem big to you? Then make sure that God knows how big it looks to your eyes and He will treat it as such. He will never belittle it however trivial. He will not laugh at it, or at us. He never forgets how large our problems look to us." Corrie ten Boom. That was the writing in my journal today. It seemed to speak to me. Today was Keith's birthday. Marcie and Keith went out to Erie to Field and Stream and to pick up some ladder jacks Keith had found on Craig's List. Marcie was spending the day with him, while Michael stained their deck and Zoie and I stayed home and played. We lay out on a blanket and watched the clouds and imagined all the animals and things the clouds formed. That is one of our favorite things to do when the sky is right. It was a beautiful weekend and the weather had been amazing for weeks. Life was good. Sharon, a dear friend who made beautiful quilts had called Marcie to see what colors I liked and made me a spectacular quilt to bring with me to chemo. I didn't know why I would need a quilt, but it was stunning. My chemo would start this week, so I'd find out. I don't know if I'm nervous or not. I couldn't stop thinking about it, but it didn't seem to make me afraid. I believe I was experiencing a peace that only God gives. I was just taking one day at a time, and for now, and that was enough.

Psalms 34:4: "I sought the Lord and He answered me; He delivered me from all my fear." Tuesday was my first day of chemo. That was a verse in my Bible reading that morning. God was with me. Keith drove me there and sat with me while I got hooked up with my new port. He watched them do it and told me to never look at the needle they put in there. I made a point to follow that advice the whole way through. I got several bags of medicine before I got the chemo. One was for nausea, one was a steroid, I don't know what the others were, but one made my legs really restless. It was all I could do to sit in the chair. I imagined the medicine going into my veins and eating up all the cancer like little Pacmen. It was a mental picture I would play over and over again each time I got the bag of chemo.

Once I got the medicine started and the nurses had checked on me more times than I could count, I told Keith to go home. I had to sit for a couple hours and there was no sense him sitting there, watching me. Besides, *Alaskan Bush People* was doing a marathon on TV, and I loved that show. See! God even took care of my television! I felt a great peace starting this. I felt like I was finally starting the fight; today, we defeat cancer. The nurses were so compassionate. It wasn't as scary a place as I first thought. It wasn't really pleasant, more clinical, but it wasn't bad. I also figured out why I needed that quilt. They put this stuff in your system at room temperature, and it cools you down a lot. I was freezing and so thankful that I had my quilt!

The next day, I woke up feeling good. I didn't seem to have any side effects from the chemo. So far. My Bible reading from today included Psalm 91:15–16, "He shall call upon me and I will answer him. I will be with him in trouble. I will deliver him and honor him with long life. I will satisfy him and show him my salvation." I sent this letter to everyone on my prayer chain list:

> I got my first chemotherapy treatment yesterday. It is one of 4 that I will be taking to begin with. This is very strong stuff. They don't want me to even leave the house until they can do a white count next Wednesday to see how I'm tolerating it.
>
> I am tolerating it amazingly well. I had no nausea, no pain, no numbness (three of the biggest, usual problems)
>
> I slept like a baby last night and I'm fine today. THAT is answered prayer and God has been so faithful to me. I feel everyone's prayers and His presence near whenever I get a little nervous or scared of the next steps.
>
> He is teaching me to take one day at a time and be thankful for the wonderful things going on today. Not to worry at all about what's coming tomorrow. Today was enough to handle. God's got me ☺. He has given me wonderful, praying friends. You are part of this latest answered prayer. Thank you.
>
> I am so grateful to each person who is lifting me up in prayer to God. He is answering those prayers by taking away the worry and the problems that could come with this chemo. Thank you, thank you, thank you for your prayers!!
>
> Jamie

"I sought the Lord and He answered me; He delivered me from all my fears." (Ps 34:4). I kept reminding myself of this verse.

Today was Thursday. The day of the Jamestown Transportation Clambake. Marlene (a dear friend of mine) and Dawn (the gal who'd gone through cancer a year before me) were both on the board with me. It was the three of us. I couldn't be around that many people, so I asked some of my coworkers from Erie to come down and take my place. Everyone I worked with was so willing to fill in whenever I needed help. It really is an amazing group of people I work with. I had a cake delivered for Marlene's birthday and everyone had their picture taken around the cake to text me, saying they all missed me. How sweet! Dawn dropped off what was left of the cake after the party. I wasn't eating anything with sugar in it, but it sure was sweet of her to bring it to me. Today, I woke up really tired and had been exhausted all day long. I wasn't sick, just really tired. Tomorrow I would talk to the surgeon I hoped would be doing my surgery. I was excited to meet him.

Friday, Keith drove me to Erie to meet with Dr. Engel. What a wonderful man! I asked him if he was a Christian. He said his grandpa was a preacher, his uncle was a preacher, his mother wrote Christian literature, and if he hadn't become a surgeon, he probably would have been a preacher. He believed. Thank you, God, for leading me here to this man! He was the first person besides Dr. Conner that said he wasn't worried about the 25 growth rate. He said if it was 75, he'd be worried. He said my doctors had done exactly what he would be doing and I was good. He asked who I wanted for a plastic surgeon to work on me during the surgery with him. I didn't know anyone, but he mentioned a man about my age, and I said him! I'd meet him later.

For now, I was going to take the chemo and come back to him when I was just about done with all of that, and we'd start looking at the surgery dates. If all went well, that would be around the end of the year. If the chemo didn't react; it didn't matter—I wouldn't need him.

But I felt like God was here and I was going to get well. If my plans and God's plans weren't in alignment, I'd know soon enough. Until then, I was planning to get better. My journal had Psalm

46:1 written on today's page: "God is our refuge and strength, an ever-present help in trouble."

Saturday, I woke up with an upset stomach. I drank some ginger ale and it seemed to settle my stomach a bit. My mind kept racing around all the things that could happen, and God kept bringing me back to the fact that he loves me and he is sufficient. He was helping me stay calm through this. I felt a little out of control and I had to keep remembering to only take one day at a time. Today was the only day that mattered. The ginger ale seemed to help a little bit, and Marcie had gone and gotten me some ginger tea. Between the two, I felt better by dinner time.

This was the first week I didn't get to church. I wouldn't be going again until my chemo was done. Too many people; too many germs. Dad had a bad morning downstairs, and he didn't go either. Today, Keith took down the pool in the backyard. We'd had it for six or seven years, and I just couldn't think about closing it or opening it again, so we decided to take it down. He got everything down and cleaned up the yard where it was and spread new dirt. By next summer, you'd never know it was there. I sat on the back deck and watched him work. I could get used to this!

Monday was Labor Day. I felt pretty good. Zoie and I sat on the porch and played our guitars and sang Bible songs. Marcie had gotten Zoie a small guitar for Christmas. She didn't know how to play it, but we strummed away and sang our hearts out. It was a wonderful day!

Tuesday, I was feeling really tired again. I worked until three and then took a nap. I was having some stomach issues. I am choosing to believe that God would answer my prayers for healing. I was waiting patiently but expectantly on the Lord. This was going to be a long, hard journey.

My journal said: "Our responsibility is to keep knocking at God's door . . . to keep believing God will answer our prayers . . . patiently but expectantly wait on the Lord." (Thelma Wells).

Wednesday, I got a low white count report—asked everyone to pray for me. I am so thankful for praying friends.

> Just found out that my white count is still below normal even with the shot, so pray it'll come up enough for me to have my next chemo ☺. Thank you for your prayers!! ☺ I need to be really careful not to catch something that's going around because I don't have anything to fight it with.
>
> I'm not feeling bad, I just need to keep my white count up so I can continue treatments. Your prayers are working and God is in control. :0)
>
> I love you all for praying!
>
> Thanks! Jamie

Keith got the flu that night. I was truly relying on God now. I didn't want to catch this and not be able to keep on my chemo schedule. They told me staying on schedule was very important with cancer like mine. We had to stay on schedule so it didn't get time in between treatments to change and grow. I started to get a little bit crazy with the germs; spraying every surface and doorknob I could think of, and Keith started sleeping in the office in a recliner.

I woke up Thursday more tired than I'd ever been in my life. I got weepy by ten thirty. Stopped working by eleven and took a nap. I felt better after lunch and finished my calls before I quit. I wanted to be able to work, but I could see that I was going to have to be really careful about anything else if I was going to have enough energy to do that.

I was going to have to make sure I got some food and lots of water and more sleep than I'd ever gotten. That's going to have to be my new routine if I wanted to be able to keep working. I'd make it work. I needed to work. Not just to keep my mind off what I was going through but also to be able to support us! I was hoping to get through this without losing my house. I knew my company was wonderfully supportive, but I couldn't ask them to carry me this whole way. I needed to do a respectable job. I'd make this work one way or the other.

Keith still wasn't feeling well, but he went out to get me gift cards for my sister's birthday card. He has been so wonderful to me. I don't think I could have made it this far if he hadn't been there with me every step of the way. Helping me when I needed and just being silently supportive when I didn't. I love that man. I am blessed. Thank you, God, for my amazing family.

Psalm 107:19: "Then they cried out to the Lord in their trouble and He saved them out of their distresses. He sent His word and healed them." Today's verse.

Friday was a good day. I woke up feeling stronger. I actually ate and worked without any trouble. I think more sleep and more water was the key. Keith was finally starting to feel better too.

I woke up Saturday to rain, but I felt wonderful, normal even! Wow! Thank you, God. I did some laundry, did the dishes, and ate three meals. Today was a great day! Dad had a great day too. Thank you, God, for a wonderful day. I don't take them for granted anymore!

Sunday was still a great day. I even canned up a double batch of spaghetti sauce. It was wonderful to feel so good! We had Norm and Brenda over for dinner. Spaghetti, of course.

The whole weekend was great! I felt good on Monday too. Zoie stopped over before school to visit from 7:00 to 7:30 a.m. She was such a blessing to me. She knew I was sick, but we didn't really say anything about it. She kept tugging on my hair to see if it was falling out yet because we told her it probably would. I think that fascinated her.

I just didn't want her to be afraid when it did.

Tuesday was my second round of chemo. Then I'd be halfway through the "red devil." Thank you, God, for carrying me. No problems again this time. Keith actually just dropped me off and came to pick me up when I called him just before I was done. Felt good all day. Keith was working on a roll bar for his tractor so he didn't ever have another accident like the one he just had. Good.

James 1:2–3: "Count it all joy my brethren when you meet trials of various kinds, for you know that the testing of your faith produces steadfastness." Today's verse.

I woke up at 4:00 a.m. Wednesday sick; got some ginger ale. Note to self—don't eat much on chemo days; even if you do feel good. Lesson learned.

I spent time before work with God, asking him to show me how I could use this journey to bring people to him; asking for his words if I do get the opportunity. I felt okay all day. Thank you again, God.

My washing machine broke down and repair man said it wasn't worth fixing, "Get a new one." It's always something but now little things like that don't even faze me anymore. So what? The washing machine broke. Get a new one; problem solved. No money for it? So what—charge it. Pay it later. God has taken care of us this far, he'll do it now. It's a beautiful day today, and I'm not wasting a minute of it worrying about a washing machine.

Keith was still working on his roll bar. It was good he stayed busy. He needed something to do just like I did.

They told me at the oncologist's office to drink lots of water, get plenty of sleep, and try to get some exercise in each day. I'd been trying to take a walk up until now. I'd been just walking down our driveway to the road, turning down the road to the next driveway, which just happened to be Marcie and Michaels, walking up their driveway and over to my house. It wasn't even a quarter mile, but it was getting me out and moving. Usually, someone was around and could go for this little walk with me, but today, no one was home when I decided I should get that walk in, so I decided to just do it.

I learned a very valuable lesson today. I started walking and didn't really feel right, but I made it to the road and got down to the next driveway and started feeling lightheaded. About halfway up their driveway, I just couldn't make it any farther. I sat down in the middle of the driveway to catch my breath. I could just imagine the next person home finding me passed out in the driveway. What was I thinking? I got up and walked a little bit more and sat down again. I managed to do this about six or eight times, and the last time, I was actually laying in the driveway, but I made it to our porch steps and sat with my head between my legs until my head quit spinning.

When you are out of energy and on chemo, you do not have a reserve. Don't push it. From that point forward, I took a little walk around the porch and sat in one of the chairs when I got tired and never went alone again. That was scary. I had never felt that kind of exhaustion before. How quickly I went from a healthy, active person to someone who couldn't walk a quarter of a mile without help. But I was taking little walks on the porch during the bad days, and walking farther on good ones. The sun was shining and life was good. And now I knew my limitations, and I would abide by them from now on until this was over.

I would take care not to scare my family by pushing myself too hard and getting into trouble. I loved them too much to do that to them.

Marcie had started coming over each day to straighten my kitchen and take my garbage. My mom or dad would come up stairs each day to see if I wanted to eat anything, and Keith checked on me every half hour just to be sure I didn't need any water or anything.

My hair was starting to fall out. I cried on Keith's shoulder about it. I knew that it was coming and I had two beautiful wigs: one the Zonta ladies had helped me pick out and given me and the other that Dawn had given me.

But knowing it's probably going to happen and actually having it happen are two completely different things. This was a hard weekend. I was sad about my hair and my stomach was not feeling good. I was pretty much just drinking water and trying to get a piece of toast or an egg in just because I knew I needed to eat. I'd started out way overweight, so I wasn't worried that I'd lose weight, but I didn't want to have long-lasting problems because I didn't get enough nourishment from this.

I asked Keith if he would shave my head. I couldn't stand the hair on everything. It was falling out in big chunks now. He promised he would later, but he was going to have to work up enough courage to do it. He did do it later, and I think he cried more than I did. What an awful thing to have to do . . . shave the hair off your wife's head. But in the large scope of things, it was only hair, and hopefully, it would grow back. I think it was after my hair was gone that I started being so cold, I couldn't seem to get warm. It seemed from that point forward, I wore a sweatshirt and really warm socks and turtlenecks just to get warm. I always had a blanket over my shoulders and on my lap. I had blankets piled on the bed and still shivered all night.

I got up Monday morning and showered and went to work at my desk making calls on the phone. I started to feel a little bit better and it felt good to be able to work. I had scheduled a meeting with the cancer care people. They had a program called Look Good, Feel Better. They had volunteer beauticians that helped you draw on your eyebrows and put on makeup that makes you look more healthy and peppy. I didn't feel good enough to go, so I had to cancel that. I'd try it at a later date. I worked still, but that was about it. I pretty much lay on the couch after that until I went to bed. But I was starting to feel better. Thank you, God, for all my praying friends and your sweet love that was holding me, carrying me right now through this.

I've always been weepy when I'm tired and I was really tired now. I'd be glad to get over this weepiness for a bit! I couldn't seem to talk to anyone about anything without crying. I didn't want to make people feel uncomfortable, but I just couldn't seem to stop myself from crying. I've been telling them it's just me. Everyone was patient and wonderful. I just felt so tired and weepy and thankful they just kept coming to visit even though I was an emotional train wreck.

It's good to have people visit. I'm trying to be very careful not to get sick, but it's good to see people. Val brought me some motion sickness, pressure point bracelets. She'd heard they worked for chemo patients sometimes, so she was hoping they'd help me. I think they did help a little. How thoughtful.

Keith went grocery shopping for the first time in forty years without me. He took Zoie with him. They came home with four different flavors of ice cream, several different kinds of cookies and candy, and some sprinkles. I think he spent over $100, and I honestly don't think there's a thing there I could eat! Oh, well, at least he had a good time with Zoie, though there really wasn't anything there she should eat either!

I eventually found the key. Get up, get showered, work until noon. Nap for forty-five minutes and work again until four or five. Hopefully, this would work until I could get back out in person and see my customers. We'd see. I was feeling pretty good!

The weather had been a gift and the fall colors were amazing. I was really enjoying that. I was feeling better and better the farther we get from the chemo. I'd go back on Tuesday for my next one. I felt good enough over the weekend to do some weeding in the garden. It felt wonderful to be out in the sunshine and active. What a blessing! Tonight was the blood moon. We sat out on the back deck and watched it, me, Keith, Mom, and Dad. I'd just read John Haggee's book *Four Blood Moons*. It was pretty interesting. We're living in crazy times. It's like we're watching the books of Daniel and Revelations come to life before our eyes!

I settled into a routine of getting chemo on Tuesday, feeling really punky by Friday afternoon and being pretty much down all weekend. I'd started feeling pretty good Monday and much better as the week went on, until the following Monday, when I almost felt normal, just in time to have chemo again on Tuesday. It got a little worse each time, but in the two-week cycle, I was really only down for two-and-a-half days. That was doable. I'd kind of figured it out about the time we changed formulas of chemo, and I was done with the red devil.

Just before I had the last of that formula, I had a checkup. The physician's assistant marveled at how well I was doing. My cancer was shrinking and my numbers were good (considering), and she was amazed at how well I was tolerating the treatments. She said she wished she could bottle whatever I was doing and give it to her other patients that hadn't done nearly as well as I had. I told her it was God answering all the prayers that had been sent up to him on my behalf. I told her that prayer was an incredibly powerful thing, and I believed that God was going to heal me. The hope I felt in that was so comforting. You can't put God in a bottle, but he's there for anyone who calls on him. Just wait and see what he's going to do with me!

To my prayers warriors . . .

> I also wanted to tell you about my most recent chemo on Tuesday so you can see how God is answering the prayers sent up on my behalf.
>
> Before the chemo you get a little mini check up.
>
> The nurse practitioner said she wished they could bottle up whatever I'm doing and give it to everyone because I was doing so well with this chemo. It's about the strongest chemo they have and while I've lost my hair and have a couple of days that I really don't get off the couch (looking forward to that about Friday ☺), I am doing very well through it. She said most people have lots of troubles with this one because of the strength of it. I told her it was just answered prayer. Plain and simple but powerful and amazing. I'm a walking testimony to the power of prayer and of God's protection and love.

So thank you dear friends for all your prayers. They're working! God has surely blessed me and everyone who is praying for me. I ask him every morning to bless the people who are lifting my name up to him in prayer. So I hope you're feeling His blessings!!

In my journal today: "Our God can handle even the worst that can happen to us as finite human beings. Since Christ is beside us, no troubles that life can bring need cast us adrift. This is a knowledge which can release us from lifelong bondage to fear. Catherine Marshall. AMEN!"

I had been blessed with a wonderful family and they were making it so much easier for me. Between Keith and Marcie and Mike and Mom and Dad, I was all set. They were doing everything for me. I was indeed blessed. Then add in the beautiful friends God had given us, and it was almost overwhelming how blessed we were. Thank you, God, for lining this path with such beautiful, praying friends.

I found out that one of my dear friends, Marlene, was going through cancer too. She didn't tell me until after she'd had surgery because she didn't want to add that to my plate. She had ovarian cancer. They thought they got it all, but she was going to have to have chemo too.

Several times we had it together. What a horrible thing to have to do with a friend, but we still had a good time when our treatments ended up being together. We couldn't visit the whole time because I couldn't stay awake the whole time anymore, but until it got to me, I'd wheel my little medicine bag holder into her room and sit with her. She was now on my prayer list. I was going to pray her through this too. We were both going to be cancer survivors. I don't care what the odds were, we had God, and he could handle this.

As I got to the end of the first type of chemo, the nausea started a little sooner and lasted a little longer. I found it wasn't worth it to eat salads. I'd be sick for days over a small salad. I pretty much ate eggs and oatmeal. The chemo was starting to kick my butt, so I was sure it was killing the cancer!

"Hope is the word which God has written on the brow of every man." (Victor Hugo). From my journal today.

"Do not be afraid of sudden terror nor trouble from the wicked when it comes for the Lord will be your confidence and will keep your foot from being caught." (Ps. 3:25,)

One of my customers asked me to write something for a cancer benefit they were having at her church. This is what I wrote and I sent along a picture of me in my scarf.

> "I'm sorry Mrs. Richir, it is cancer." It was the call I couldn't believe I was receiving. I've always been lucky and blessed and happy. This can't be right. "I'm sorry, could you repeat that?" I asked the doctor.
>
> He repeated the sentence but added, "But we don't think it's primary breast cancer, we think it may be metastasized from another origin. We'll run more tests and let you know on Monday."
>
> Until this call, I didn't think a sentence could be worse than I'm sorry, it is cancer, but with a few added words I've been given a potential death sentence.
>
> I turned to tell my husband but couldn't get any words out. My world had just been completely flipped upside down. I covered my face and started to weep. Until two minutes ago I never would have imagined my prayers would be, please God, let it be breast cancer. Who could imagine the prognosis of breast cancer would be an answered prayer? Certainly not me. I'm the healthy one. I'm the one who was able to step up when my husband got sick 27 years ago and was never able to work again. I'm the strong one; the blessed with good health one. This can't be

happening. There's some kind of mistake. I'd just had a clean mammogram a couple months earlier. They'll call back in a few minutes and apologize for the clerical error and I'll go about my healthy, merry way.

But they didn't call back. I spent that Friday evening vacillating from sheer panic to disbelief, pleading with God to take this away. It just can't be.

My mind wandered to all the worst case scenarios. I kept thinking of my precious five year old granddaughter Zoie and how much I wanted to live to see her grown. Please God. Please.

But my pleas were born of panic and my prayers were disconnected and flighty. My mind was bouncing from one morbid worst case scenario to the next. It wasn't until the middle of the night that I finally realized the first of many truths God would reveal to me through this journey. I had my bible open and I was weeping and praying when the thought came to me . . . wait, stop. This panic is a waste of energy and I'm a Christian. I serve a living savior. If I truly believe God created me and He is in control, then why all this panic?

God IS in control.

God loves me enough to send His son Jesus to die for me as a sacrifice for my sins.

He knows the plans He has for me.

He is bigger than my cancer.

This didn't surprise Him the way it did me and He's got me.

That was the moment that **the peace that passes all understanding** washed over me and I realized that I was going to be OK. God had me safely tucked under His wing and no matter what, I was going to be OK.

The awesome God who created the universe and everything in it; including me had promised He would Never leave me or forsake me. I was good.

I ended up having a very aggressive form of cancer. I'm about half way through my chemo and then I will have surgery and probably radiation afterwards. But I'm OK. God has answered so many prayers along this difficult journey for me already. I can see His hand in so many answers to prayers and I know He will carry me through to the end of this cancer journey and also this life.

I have claimed victory over this cancer through my savior Jesus Christ and I thank God every day for His love. I know He has a plan for me and I pray that He will reveal what my path is and I will walk faithfully in it.

Our God is a help in times of trouble and He's got us—No matter what—He's got us. What an amazing God we serve.

Connie read this at their church benefit with a picture of me in the scarf on the overhead screen. She said it had an impact on the people; there wasn't a dry eye in the place. To God be the glory. If talking about what I'm going through can help someone, it makes my journey seem somehow worth the struggle. And it was becoming a struggle.

I seemed to have more and more difficulty getting through the days with any energy. I'd still get up, shower, go to my desk, and work, but that was it. I was exhausted, but I didn't sleep as soundly as I needed, so I wasn't getting the rest I needed. It was becoming harder and harder to eat enough. But compared to the other patients, I was doing amazingly well, so I was thankful. I was truly thankful that I had a job I could do for a time at my desk at home. This couldn't be permanent, but for now, we could make it work. God had provided everything I needed, including a company that had compassion, and wonderful people who were helping me out with anything I needed help on. I worked directly with Craig and Bobby. They'd been my sales support, and now they were really helping me out. If a customer needed an in-person visit, they were doing that for me. Fortunately, most of my customers knew what I was going through, and they were working with me until this trial was over. But Bobby and Craig were there if I needed them

We were going through a long stretch of incredibly beautiful weather. I really appreciated that. I'd make a point each day to sit outside for a couple minutes to enjoy it. Usually my mom would sit with me and we'd talk. It was a precious time for me. Mom was amazing when it came to keeping my mind on positive, good things. We'd sit and watch Dad planting something until he got too tired and came and sat with us.

I am truly blessed to have them and they have helped me so much through this trial.

Monday, October 13, was the last of my red devil chemo. From this point forward, I'd get a different formula. I would be halfway through after today. It was a milestone and I was celebrating! Well, the celebration was mostly an attitude. I was halfway through this! Yay!

The cancer was shrinking; we were kicking cancer's butt and I was halfway through this part of the journey. It was a good start.

I was celebrating making it halfway through my chemo and thinking about my sweet Aunt Audrey who had done this twice! I thought about her and what she went through. I missed her a lot too. Mom and Aunt Audrey were so close; I can't imagine how much Mom missed her. Mom had also helped Audrey through her chemo with her upbeat, positive ways. Mom is the last of her family in her generation and she sometimes wonders why she was the last. I think it is because she is such a positive influence and a voice for trusting in God. He is certainly still using her to help me through this!

I found an article in the doctor's office about alkaline foods. They keep your body from getting acidic, which may have a link to cancer growth. The foods were common, so I wrote them down. I was going to go back to these. It couldn't hurt.

Fruits, green vegetables, peas, nuts, carrots, broccoli, celery, green beans, tomatoes, apples, bananas, berries, cantaloupes, grapes, lemons, oranges, peaches, pears, and watermelon.

But for right now, I was relying heavily on the people who are praying me through the day. Eating had become something I just made myself do because I knew I needed to for strength. I lost a bunch of weight, but I'd come prepared for this battle. I could lose a bunch more and they wouldn't be worried about me. One good thing about being fat!

I was getting up, hoping the day will go fast, so I could check it off as another day closer to this treatment being over. But we're getting there. Hopefully the next type of chemo would be a bit easier. We'd see.

The nurses kept asking me each time I have my treatment if I'm noticing what they call "chemo fog." I kept telling them I hadn't noticed it yet. I was telling Marcie about it and she said I definitely did have it! Oh, dear! It's so bad I didn't even *know* I had it! Oh, well, you gotta laugh!

This was the week I started the new type of chemo. I was hoping it would be a little easier on my poor stomach! Ugh.

The new chemo was a little easier on my stomach as it turned out, but it came with a whole new set of difficulties. It was a trade. I'd come home from the chemo, go directly to the bathroom, pull my dressing table chair up to hang onto, and pull the waste basket up onto my lap. Then I'd spend the next ten minutes—which felt like ten hours—violently spewing out the results of the poison we'd just put into my body to kill the cancer from every orifice. I'd lay on the bathroom floor for about ten minutes after that to build up enough strength to make it to the recliner. I'd rest there for about half an hour and then I'd be fine. I'd actually be good until about Friday evening. Once Friday evening got here, I couldn't even make it to the bathroom without help. I found myself waking up looking at the ceiling in the hallway a couple times on the way to the bathroom, and realized that I shouldn't make the trip anymore without assistance. I'm lucky I didn't break my neck when I passed out! I'd be down until Sunday night when I would start feeling better. From Friday until Sunday night, I was lucky to keep down water. But I actually felt better than the first half of my chemo. I was able to eat. I didn't eat much more than an egg or some oatmeal or maybe a slice of toast, but I was able to eat, so I was feeling stronger and I was sleeping better. I could do this! Thank you, God, for giving me everything I needed to get through this. Thank you that Keith was here to help me when I couldn't make it on my own. And thank you for my sweet prayer warriors who were holding me up to you.

HI,

I've finished up the first half of my chemo treatments and have started the second. This new one came with it's own set of issues, but I'm doing OK with it. Only three more treatments! Thank you all for your prayers, they are what's gotten me through this. I can't say enough about how much they mean to me.

I've learned so many things on this journey. One of the lessons has been how much each of you means to me. Having you with me on this journey was no accident. God had our lives intersect for a purpose and I am blessed to have each one of you. Thank you for being a faithful, praying friend.

Another huge lesson has been the peace God gives you when you're passing through a storm. It does pass all understanding and I am so thankful for it. Without it I would be just a puddle on the floor. I hope none of you ever has a reason to search for that peace, but know that it's there should you ever need it.

I can finally see the light at the end of this dark tunnel and that view is what keeps me smiling! Thank you to each one of you for getting me here. Thank you from the bottom of my heart!

Jamie
Psm 46:1

Some ladies in a sewing circle made quilts for all the chemo patients. I forgot the quilt Sharon gave me one day, and they brought me in another one and said it matched my sweater, and I could keep it! Oh my goodness! Another beautiful quilt! I have made one quilt in my lifetime so far, and it takes a lot of time and concentration to make one of these beautiful creations! I was feeling so special that day when I came home with a quilt and had one folded up on the living room couch that I used every day. Some people are just so compassionate and filled with incredible love and generosity. I would have never thought to do something like that! I was humbled by it. This was another experience I never would have had without cancer. I was learning compassion—from the receiving end—the hard way.

Life continued on as I underwent chemo. Friends and family came by to visit. Coleen came faithfully to clean my house for me. Zoie had started kindergarten and was going through all the firsts that entailed. Keith kept busy getting everything ready for winter. I made my daily telephone calls and worked some lists for new business, all while trying to keep things as normal as possible. Mom and Dad came upstairs every day that I couldn't make it down to visit them. Marcie and Michael came by every day to see what I needed and Marcie would do the dishes Keith left in the sink. I was blessed and getting spoiled!

I was always cold now. I kept really thick socks and lots of layers on all the time with either my wig or hats always. Even with all the extra clothes, I was always cold.

I was also starting to have a bit of trouble with my feet. They called it neuropathy, and it was common in cancer patients that take strong chemo. It may go away after I'm done with the chemo. Not a real big problem; it just always felt like I had wadded up socks stuck under my feet. Turns out it was just my feet and I couldn't really feel them anymore. As long as I wore shoes all the time, I didn't notice as much. It was when I went barefoot that I'd slap my feet when I walked because I couldn't tell when they were hitting the floor.

I was getting used to a bunch of stuff these days. I usually wore a soft cotton turban-like hat to bed to keep my head warm all night. One particular night, the hat must have fallen off and I got up to use the bathroom. I walked into the room and turned on the soft light. When I looked up into the bathroom mirror, I saw this bald old man in the mirror. It just about scared me to death and I backed up and said, "Oh!" At that instant, I realized that the old man had done exactly the same thing and it wasn't an old man at all, it was me! My hat had evidently fallen off while I was sleeping. I laughed until I cried and then I went to bed and cried myself to sleep. I'd think more about that tomorrow, and tomorrow, I will laugh about it, but that night I needed to cry.

My dad had a cancer marker test and his numbers were down to just about nothing! Thank you, God! We had been praying that Dad would get a good summer, and now we were into the fall, and he was doing even better!

I got another side effect from this new chemo. It was just starting. It was little tiny pains all over. It was like swimming in a piranha pond. Little stabbing pains all over. Horrible! I called the doctors, and the nurses said it was nerve endings and to take aspirin. I couldn't get enough relief from the pain to sleep, but I wasn't sick to my stomach, so that was good! It only lasted two or three days after each treatment, so it wasn't unbearable. Or at least it wasn't unbearable for very long!

Halloween came. Dear friends from work, Erin and Andy, came by to visit with their little guy, Jacob. I was still pretty weak from the new side effects of the chemo, but it sure was wonderful to see them! I had so many sweet friends from work and these two had become very dear to me. I had come to love them.

Veterans Day; chemo day. Only two more after this one. I'm getting there! I talked for a bit with sweet Dr. Ibabao. We also talked about God and miracles and how God was going to give me one. I told him to just watch and see the amazing things God was doing to do with me! He just smiled.

I overheard him talking about one of his patients to his nurse today outside my door. He was telling his nurse to tell them not to do something for his patient in the hospital because it would cause him pain, and there was no sense doing that when he was dying. I bet he would love to see God give me a miracle after all the people he has had to watch die. He is a lovely man; this has to take a toll on him.

I woke up to the first snow of the season on November 14. It's always magical to see the first snow cover the ground each year. I was up most of the night, not feeling well at all; it was the weekend after chemo.

I turned to my Bible through the night and James 1:12 spoke to me: "Blessed is a man who endures trials, because when he passes the test he will receive the crown of life that He has promised to those who love Him."

I woke up on Monday and felt pretty good. After work, I went to a Look Good, Feel Better meeting at the hospital. I'd missed one earlier when I just wasn't up to it and had to reschedule. It was put on by the Cancer Society for the purpose of helping ladies going through cancer treatments feel better about their bald, eyelash-less selves. I was skeptical. But I went because I thought anything to perk up my looks couldn't hurt. After mistaking myself for an old man in the mirror, I figured I needed all the help I could get! It was wonderful!

I was there with four other ladies who were going through breast cancer treatments. Not one of us had a single hair on our bodies. I can't say that I missed having hair anyplace else, but I did miss it on my head and my eyebrows and my eyelashes. I missed it in my nose too. I didn't realize how quickly snot runs out of your nose without it! Five seconds and it's into your mouth! Yuck!

We all got together, and by the end of the evening, we'd all cried and told a little bit of our sad stories, and these beautiful volunteer ladies helped us learn how to put real-looking eyebrows on and light up our faces a little bit. They showed us how to make scarves into turbans and just all kinds of fun, girly stuff. They were so sweet! And we all left there with a makeup bag full of incredible makeup! The kind you get at a BonTon counter, not at Walmart! Nice stuff! I left there feeling like I was pretty again. It was really nice. I did lose the only eyebrow I had left in the process though. The gal asked me if I wanted to learn how to paint on my eyebrows. I told her I'd do it on one side, but I had one eyebrow hair left on the other side, and I was protecting it! By the end of the night, I'd drawn over the eyebrow hair and it came off in the process. It was inevitable, and we all laughed at the silly things we cling to while we're losing our hair.

The opening day of deer season was upon us. This is usually a big darn deal at the Richir Ranch. Keith usually has a bunch of guys and they plan where they're going and who's doing what. This year it was on Saturday, very unusual. Keith just had his nephew and a friend come with him this year. He kept it low key so I could rest. It was the off week from chemo, and I was feeling pretty good. I took Zoie and her babysitter over to see the Santa Parade. We were a little early so we walked across the street to the library to see Sue, Betty and Lori. The gals at the library had sent me cards and were praying for me so I thought since I was so close I'd pop in and say thank you. They were all friends and I tried to stop by whenever I had a minute. I just loved visiting with them. I didn't read as much as I used to since my eye surgery, but I never wanted to lose touch with those girls! From there we walked a little way down Main Street. I realized when we got there that it had been too far and I was out of energy. I wouldn't have enough energy to stand and get back to my car and I'd brought the kids!

I was leaning on the front of one of the stores, and the gentlemen came out and asked if I'd like a chair. He moved some stuff off a bench he had in front of his store and I sat there. He'd noticed that I was leaning heavily on the wall and I think he recognized the look we all have—those of us without hair and eyebrows. He said he had gone through chemo twice but was now cancer–free, and he knew what I was going through. What a beautiful thing to do. I usually breeze through life not noticing things around me. I hoped when I get done with this I would take the time to notice what's near me. I was going to start praying that God would give me his eyes so I can see if there's anything I could do for those around me. I was learning so many lessons on my journey through cancer. One of the biggest is how wonderful people are to each other. I know the news shows horrible things, and I know there are a lot of horrible things, but there is so much good in people!

There's an old saying, "There's so much good in the worst of us and so much bad in the best of us, it ill behooves any of us to find fault with the rest of us." Nobody knows what someone is going through, so we should all just try to be kind to each other. To help when we see a need and to be actively looking to find that need. I'm learning.

That night I woke up dreaming that the cancer was getting bigger again. What a horrible dream! I whispered out loud, "Satan, get thee behind me!" Gramma Eunice used to say that all the time whenever she was troubled or tempted, so I figured now was a good time to say it myself. I said a long prayer for God to strengthen me and went back to sleep. A storm had blown in cold weather and when I woke up, it was winter.

Corie, that dear artist friend of mine, came and brought me a beautiful painting she'd taught in her last evening painting class. It was a vase with pink flowers and a Bible verse traveling around the vase. Ephesians 6:10: "Be strengthened in the Lord and His mighty power." God reminding me again that he was holding me through this. I was okay.

Zoie also brought me a beautiful shawl that her Nonny had made for me. Michael's mom was incredible at crochet. Both of these ladies had been used by God to assure me that I was okay. He loved me and he'd send people to encourage me. What an amazing God we serve! I felt so loved . . . again, people being so incredibly kind to others in need. I had just never been the one in need. I never realized how incredible it felt to be on the receiving end.

The next day was Monday and I'd slept really well through the night. Probably the best I'd slept since this whole thing started. What a difference a night of good sleep can make! I felt great both Monday and Tuesday and got all my work and then some done those days. I was on fire!

Wednesday was chemo day. After this one, only one more left. We were getting there. Slowly but surely, we were making it with God's help and my family carrying me along. Marlene was there getting her chemo when I arrived. We sat together for a bit and visited. It was a nice thing to be with a friend. Not so nice to be getting chemo together, but somehow, it was easier to have company. I got too tired to stay in her room, so I couldn't stay the whole time with her, and she got done quite a bit before me. Marlene was already a dear friend, but I don't think you share chemo with too many people and this was a bond we would never forget. Or maybe it was all the prayers we were praying for each other. I don't know. I just know that I'll always love Marlene.

I will always love Coleen too! She just kept coming to clean my house and make sure everything was in order. She'd come at least every other week and spend the whole day doing an amazing job. Everything was dusted and mopped and the toilets were scrubbed. All the dishes were done and the sheets were changed and the laundry was done. What an incredible thing to do for someone. She was ever faithful and tireless! And she was one of my greatest sources for words from God. She always had a Bible verse or a thought about a verse God had given her for me. She was amazing.

My journal said, "Each of us may be sure that if God sends us on stony paths, He will provide us with strong shoes, and He will not send us out on any journey for which He does not equip us well." (Alexander MacLaren). I feel like Keith and my family and sweet friends like Coleen were my strong shoes. I was ready for this journey!

This week, my chemo was the day before Thanksgiving, so I had to go to the hospital for the Neulasta shot on Thanksgiving Day. I actually had everyone at our house for Thanksgiving. I put the turkey in at 8:00 a.m. with Keith's help and went to the hospital for my shot.

A thankful heart this Thanksgiving :0)
I wanted to take a minute to thank each of
you again for your continued prayers. I know it

seems like it's been a very long time (to me too :0) But your prayers are being heard and answered by God and I am eternally grateful for each and every one of you who lift my name up to Him. He is an amazing, loving, prayer answering God and I am living proof of that!!

This new chemo has its own challenges. I seem to recover a little quicker with this cocktail, but I am a little sicker right off the bat and the first time I experienced horrible nerve pain. About the time I get this all figured out, I'll be done – Thank GOD!!

Last week before I went in for the next round, God gave me a verse and reaffirmed to me that He was going to heal me of this and He was here with me in this struggle. It was another incredible moment. I've experienced so many of those moments since this journey began. Maybe Tim McGraw knew what he was talking about in his song about "living like you're dying". But God again calmed my soul. I think the journey was getting long and I was getting tuckered out. That's a dangerous place to be because doubt starts creeping in. But God gave me this verse Psm 40:1-3

I waited patiently for the Lord and He inclined to me and heard my cry. He brought me up out of the pit of destruction, out of the miry clay, and He set my feet upon a rock making my footsteps firm. He put a new song in my mouth, a song of praise to our God; many will see and fear and will trust in the Lord.

This Thanksgiving, I just wanted you to know that I am so thankful for each and every one of you. Thank you from the bottom of my

heart for your continued prayers. I think of
you often and thank God for you. I hope your
Thanksgiving is blessed with family and friends
that you make beautiful memories with. You
have been a true blessing to me.

Everyone came to the house; since I couldn't really go any place, they came to me. And they all brought stuff and fixed everything and cleaned up too. I was so thankful to God for giving me this Thanksgiving, but I was too overwhelmed with thankfulness to get the blessing out before dinner. Zoie wanted to have each of us say what we were thankful for. She was thankful for breathing and for her mom and dad. I think she was just getting over a nasty cold and stuffy nose, but I cried all the way through it as quietly as I could. Such simple, wise words. They had a completely different meaning to me. I was thankful for each breath God would give me.

Every day, yes every breath, is such a gift, and I never realized how precious each breath was until I realized that I didn't know how many more I might have left! Today was a gift and I knew how blessed I was to be here now. I was thankful for my Savior, Jesus Christ, who is seated at the right hand of God right now, interceding on my behalf and has been so present to me through comfort, peace, and answered prayer. I was thankful for Keith, Mom, Dad, Marcie, Michael, and Zoie who so lovingly looked after me day after day and encouraged me when I get down and weepy. I was so blessed and I was so thankful!

This had been especially hard on Keith. He had been right there with me through all of it. He had seen all my weakness and my weepiness and how scared I'd get until I remembered that God had me and I was not alone in this. He had held me when I cried, driven me every place I needed to go, walked me to the bathroom when I couldn't make it myself. I knew he was a good man before, but when I saw how wonderful he could be, I felt blessed. Thank you, God, for all the amazing, supportive people you have put in my life. I was blessed beyond measure and I was so thankful.

I don't think I'd ever been as truly thankful as I was that year. How funny that you have to almost lose everything to see how much you really have. I was learning so much! I read something today that said, "There is a deep peace that grows out of illness." (Frank C. Laubach). I believe that. I had been a Christian since I was a child, old enough to make a profession, but I had never walked closer to him or relied more fully on him then since I had become sick. I had never felt such profound peace as I had now that I'd been walking with him and relying completely on him.

Sick, sick, sick. Thanksgiving and chemo do not go together. I don't care how careful you are. They do not mix. Ugh.

The following week, I met with Dr. Engel, the surgeon who would be doing my mastectomy. He would schedule the surgery with Dr. Garcia, the plastic surgeon, for the end of the month if he could. I asked to have all of it done at once and have it done on December 22, so I'd be done before Christmas. He was going to wait until after the last chemo and see how strong I was, and then he'd let me know, but it'd probably be after Christmas. We would likely have to wait two to three weeks after chemo to do the surgery so I could get stronger before it. We'd be looking at December 29 or January 5, most likely. One more chemo to go. I asked him if I really needed the last one . . . hoping. Absolutely, yes, I do. I was almost done with the hardest part, I thought. I could do whatever I had to do. God was holding me now. I wasn't even walking in the sand, he was carrying me now.

Wednesday, December 9, 2015—the day of my last chemo. Thank you, God, for getting me here. I never missed a chemo, I didn't need a blood transfusion, and I'd made it through on schedule. It was truly a miracle and I was thanking God. When I got home, my sister Janet had flowers delivered to me in celebration of my last chemo treatment. Mom made me mac-n-cheese for dinner to celebrate!

The next day was Zoie's sixth birthday, and Aunt Jill and Uncle Steven bought her pie face. What a hoot! We all got pie faced with whipped cream and had so much fun. We laughed and laughed. What a great day.

That weekend was my last weekend being sick from chemo. I could do this standing on my head. I was almost smiling while I was sick because I knew it was the last chemo. I knew we were kicking cancer's butt, and soon we would be cutting what was left of it out of my body. The miracle God had given me, the one I was already thanking him for would be realized. Amen!

I had a test coming up in Olean. Keith would drive me this time. I didn't see any customers this time. I was too close to surgery and didn't want to catch anything before then.

The weather was still in the fifties. We were experiencing unseasonably mild weather. The following week, I met with Dr. Garcia. That whole visit was an answer to prayer. He was a strong Christian man too. Both doctors who would be working on me were Christian men. I felt so safe. I felt I was on the exact path that God had paved for me. My surgery was scheduled for December 29.

Not before Christmas, but probably a good thing. I could enjoy Christmas and not be recovering from major surgery.

A friend sent me an email with some thoughts:

"Cancer may have started this fight, but I will finish it."

"You never know how strong you are until being strong is the only choice you have."

"Feed your faith and your fears will starve to death."

I liked those.

I actually got my Christmas letter out:

Christmas 2015

Wow, have we learned a lot about living this year! I've learned some little life lessons, like it takes about 2.5 seconds when your nose starts running until it ends up in your mouth when you have no nose hairs. :0)

And some bigger lessons, like the compassion nurses show to their patients who are going through chemotherapy is like medicine and it matters because it makes everything easier for their patients. Nursing is a calling not a job.

You never really know how wonderful your husband is until you're bald and sick and sad or grumpy or crying all the time and he just keeps doing everything he can to make things better for you.

Daughters are a gift from God. Grand daughters are an amazing, additional gift from God.

To have your Mom and Dad nearby is also a gift from God.

Cards from friends and family make your day better and their prayers make your life easier. Lifting your name up to God in their prayers is truly the MOST they can do for you.

Every day is a gift; don't waste it. Find something to be happy about each day and thank God for that thing.

Nothing that happens to you surprises God or is bigger than God or is more than God can handle. He is enough and He's got you. No matter what the outcome, God is in control.

There really is a peace that passes understanding that God gives us and it's amazing.

From our house to yours this Christmas season, we wish you the Peace that only God can give; the peace that was born in a stable that first Christmas Day; the peace that comes from asking Jesus into your life as Lord.

May you come to understand the true meaning of Christmas this year and if you already know it, may you rest in that peace this holiday season.

We love you—Merry Christmas.

Keith and Jamie

Christmas Eve, we looked for a church locally that was having a Christmas Eve service. I'd really missed going to church for the past several months. We ended up at the little church I grew up in. Falconer First Baptist Church. It was very nice, and I knew many of the people still attending there because I grew up with them!

Christmas was an amazing season this year. I saw everything differently. I wasn't overwhelmed with the busy-ness of it, I was over-joyed with the beauty of it. People seemed so thoughtful. The weather seemed magical and not messy. It was just straight-up beautiful. We live in the snow belt, so Christmas is almost always white and cold. The mild weather held and we got some amazingly warm days.

Marcie took me shopping; I wrapped presents, friends came to visit. It was all wonderful. Pastor Gordy and Jean took us out to dinner, and Jean made me some of her delicious bread! Yum! The Wednesday before Christmas was sixty degrees! Life was good. I had my pre-surgery tests at the local hospital Christmas Eve. Christmas Day was fifty degrees! Everyone at our house, me, Keith, Mom, and Dad walked over to Marcie's house to watch Zoie open presents and have breakfast. Michael's family had all spent the night so they were there to watch. It was a houseful and it was Christmas magic!

Monday, I met with both Dr. Engle and the anesthesiologist. My surgery was scheduled for the next day. I needed to be there at twelve thirty.

Hi,

I'm having my surgery tomorrow; probably late morning to early afternoon. I just wanted all of you who've prayed so faithfully for me to know so you can pray me through this next step ☺. I truly appreciate all your prayers. They are what's gotten me through this far! Thank you from the bottom of my heart for your prayers ☺

Jamie

Keith, Marcie, Mom, Dad, and even Pastor Gordy and Jean were all there to pray over me and wish me well. I got the fast track in because the surgery ahead of me didn't take as long as they thought, so they were waiting for me when I arrived. I spoke with Dr. Engel and then Dr. Garcia came in and drew all over my chest . . . a map of things to come. And off I went into surgery. Goodbye cancer. Thank you, God, for getting me here. Finally I was getting rid of that cancer that had controlled my life for the past six months.

I got into surgery at 1:00 p.m. and got out of recovery and into my room around 7:00 p.m., so they told me. I had a tissue-saving mastectomy on my left side with reconstruction and reduction surgery on the right side. I wasn't really with it when I got up to my room

The doctor had talked to Keith and Marcie and Mom and Dad after the surgery was finished. He believed he got all the cancer. There was cancer in the centinal node and seven of the lymph nodes. He took eight before they found one without cancer and tested ten more just to be sure they got enough of a margin. During the surgery, the doctor had to damage a nerve to get to the cancer, and I would have permanent numbness under my left arm and across the left side of my chest. But all in all, it was a successful surgery. They would know more when the complete pathology report came back from the surgery. Mom and Dad and Gordy and Jean left after the doctor's report.

Home was an hour's drive and I knew Marcie and Keith were both exhausted. So I sent them home even though they wanted to stay. They were back the next morning at 8:00 a.m. to pick me up to go home. It seemed like that wasn't enough time to be there, considering everything I'd been through, and considering how cut up I was. As it turned out, the fact that I had so many holes in me was the very reason the doctor wanted me home as quickly as he could get me there. There is a high risk of infections in situations like mine, so home was the better option.

So home, we went. I was on some pain medication to get there which made the bumps on the drive easier to handle. Marcie drove her van both ways, and it was a very smooth ride, which also helped. I was home sleeping on the couch recliner by 10:00 a.m.; less than twenty-four hours after my surgery. I only got up to go to the bathroom and slept most of the day. I did take the pain medicine that day and the first night home so I could sleep.

Thursday, my second day home, I quit taking the pain medicine because they messed up my stomach and my digestive system, and that was still a mess from the chemo. I was taking Tylenol and it really wasn't handling the pain, but I'd already resigned myself to a week of misery before it started getting better.

I had several large gauze bandages covering my incisions under a wide, stretchy cloth bandage that closed with a Velcro strip from top to bottom.

Today, those bandages underneath had to be changed. The problem was I couldn't raise my arms. I could raise my right arm a bit. Just enough to pick up my left wrist and slowly raise my left arm. My left arm didn't want to be raised at all. So this was a family exercise. As much as I'd have liked to keep how I looked a secret, I needed help. It actually took both Keith and Marcie to accomplish this job the first time. I picked up my left wrist with my right hand and slowly lifted it up enough that we could get the Velcro unhooked and get the bandages underneath replaced. I can't remember who did what, but I remember that we were all a little teary eyed before it was done; Marcie and Keith in sympathy, and me from the pain or embarrassment or exhaustion or a combination of all three. But the worst was behind me and before I knew it, this would be too. Nothing but up from here.

Friday was a very painful day. Marcie came over to paint my fingers and toes. That was a nice distraction. Michael and Zoie came over with chocolate chip cookies and Zoie stayed for a few minutes with her mom to visit. I believe this has been the longest day so far. I was really temped to take some pain medicine, but my stomach was starting to feel a little bit better, and I didn't want to go back there. I finally got to sleep that night and slept until 5:00 a.m. I was actually getting some really good sleep and that made a huge difference. I was going to be all right. God was in control and I think this was one of those times like that poem about footprints in the sand. I believe God had been carrying me through those couple days. I was in good hands, and he had given me such wonderful people to take care of me. I was truly blessed.

On Sunday after my surgery, Brenda came to visit me, and she said she felt God wanted her to tell me to trust him 100 percent, no matter what. We had a wonderful visit. I was so encouraged by her and Michael's prayers for my healing. Another beautiful couple God had put in my life. They were an amazing source of encouragement all the way through this journey. I was so glad Brenda had come to visit because on Monday, Dr. Engel called with the results. He said the cancer had invaded the skin and the muscle and had spread to the centinal node and up seven lymph nodes. He had taken eighteen nodes to give me a margin, and he thought he got it all and with radiation, we could reduce the risk of it returning to 40 percent. Forty percent seemed awfully high to me, but God had told me to trust Him 100 percent no matter what and I was going to. What perfect timing was that? What an amazing God we serve.

On Tuesday morning, January 5, God woke me up with an idea. I needed to get with the elders of the church and have a healing service. I woke up thinking of James 5:13–16, "Is anyone among you sick? Let him call for the elders of the church, and let them pray over him, anointing him with oil in the name of the Lord. And the prayer of faith will save the sick, and the Lord will raise him up."

I was going to call Pastor Gordy. I wanted to see if they would be willing to do that for me. I knew this wasn't a normal thing they did as a church, but it was biblical, and I was hoping they'd be open to it. If God said it, I wanted it!

I had an appointment with Dr. Garcia, but he didn't take the drains out because they were running too hard still. I slept most of the rest of the day. I was starting to feel human again. As a matter of fact, I got up the next day and made dinner and had my mom, dad, and Keith eat the chicken vegetable soup I made. It was very good, and I felt pretty darned accomplished to be able to do that much.

On Friday, Dr. Garcia took the drains out, and it felt *so* much better having them out, nothing pulling every time I moved. What a relief! It was a great trip to Erie too. It was January 8, and there was no rain or snow and it was forty-seven degrees! God is so good! I got home and slept all day until I got up and made mac-and-cheese for dinner. They weren't amazing meals, but it was from scratch and I was able to do it and I felt like Superwoman! Almost normal.

I had visiting nurses visit every other day to keep an eye on my wounds and make sure I was healing well and keeping everything up the way it needed to be. I felt reassured knowing they were keeping an eye on me since I came home so quickly. They were so sweet too, very encouraging.

The weather started turning to cold winter storms. I was off for two weeks to recover from the surgery. The doctors wanted me to take six weeks, but I was only in sales, so there was no stress to my job except driving around in the bad weather, and I'd take that one day at a time when the time came. I was looking forward to getting back to a normal schedule, feeling better, and getting on with life. I knew I still had radiation, another major surgery, and procedures coming up, but I wanted to get moving forward towards normal again.

I was looking forward to all that and Keith was starting to do nothing but sleep. This whole ordeal had really taken a toll on him. He was there for anything I needed, but when I didn't need him, he seemed to be sleeping all the time. I finally had a talk with him one day and told him that I was fighting with everything I had to live, and he was sleeping his life away. He either needed to find a way to get around the depression that had settled into him or he needed to talk to his doctor. He had an amazing doctor who worked with him to try to stay as healthy as he could be without spending all his time testing and doctoring. We really respected and appreciated Dr. Collins and his compassionate team of nurses and staff.

Keith was always thinking about starting some new adventure, but he was usually too cheap to buy the tools to make that happen. He thought about doing maple syrup for years and even got a small, used stove with a homemade pan on top to see if he was really interested in doing it. But it took me harassing him to finally purchase a real evaporator before it happened. He hated to spend the money. It was well worth it. Maybe not financially; you don't really make money on maple syrup, but it was worth every penny to give him something productive to do in the early spring and his maple syrup was delicious!

He had been looking at a portable sawmill for the past couple years and just hadn't been able to justify the cost. We decided he'd look into that a little more seriously. That would give him something to think about and if he decided he wanted to venture out into the sawmill business, it would take him until maple syrup season to get the mill put together. We had a plan to get Keith back among the living. I felt good about it. There was a little part of my mind that thought, What if I get cancer back, how is he going to handle all the bills? But I believed God was going to heal me and I was going to live like I believed. I wasn't going to allow the negative thoughts into my mind. Besides, God had always provided for us. If something should happen someday to me, God owned the cattle on a thousand hills. He'd take care of Keith when I was gone. God had both of us.

So we both had plans. I was getting better in a couple weeks and going back to work and Keith was going to think seriously about his sawmill.

The storms kept raging. Zoie was sleeping with her pajamas inside out with a spoon under her pillow and flushing ice cubes down the toilet each night. That was supposed to guarantee that she'd get a snow day. I'd bet Marcie was doing it too, being a teacher. I was happy that the storms and snow were coming now before I had to get back out and make calls outside. We made a horrible trip to see Dr. Engel in a blizzard. I'm so glad Keith was driving.

When I walked up to the elevator to get to the office, I saw a gal who was in surgery the same day I was there. I imagine she had something similar done. She was bent over, walking in with her husband holding her arm to keep her from falling. She looked so frail and like she was in so much pain and I felt so bad for her. I felt so incredibly blessed. I walked in by myself, upright, and feeling a little raggedy yet, but good really. I was on the mend and the cancer was gone, and I was going to be just fine. God had healed me. He had used wonderful Christian doctors and chemotherapy to do it, but God had healed me. I still had a little bit to go, but I believed the worst of it was behind me.

Dr. Engel said everything looked good. I was healing wonderfully.

Mom and Dad took us all, Keith, me, Marcie, Michael, and Zoie out to dinner at LaScala's for prime rib dinner for a pre-healing service celebration. It was delicious. It felt so good to be back out in public to do normal things. I'd been so paranoid about getting sick for so long, it just felt wonderful not to worry about it.

On January 17, 2016, the Falconer First Baptist Church had its first (at least in a very long time) healing service for me. It was an incredibly moving service. Mom and Dad were there, Marcie,

Michael, and Zoie and of course, Keith. Jill had come and so had Brenda and Mike Bunce and Val. Everyone on the board of deacons laid hands on me and prayed. Pastor Gordy anointed my head with oil and asked God to heal me in Jesus's name. I, of course, cried. I was always crying when something was emotional now.

It made me realize how hard it was for my friends to visit with me. The minute I started talking about what I was going through, I'd cry. The minute the conversation got to how bad people felt for me having to go through this, I'd cry. The minute we talked about anything the least bit emotional, I'd cry. Everything made me cry. I was just so exhausted. It was like when I was walking up the driveway and got tired when I'd first started chemo. When I got tired, there was no reserve for my strength physically and now there was no reserve emotionally. I was done in. But my friends and family just weathered the storm and sat with me, tears and all. I so appreciate how much love that took to keep coming back. As much as I tried to get through a visit without tears, I don't think it ever happened. But I'd rather have them here visiting me, maybe even squirming a little bit while I tried to get control of myself, than not have them come. I was going to remember all this so I could be there for my people should they ever need me. Thank you, God, for so many lessons through this journey. Maybe I'd be a compassionate person after all before this was done.

I left that church service knowing that God had healed me and I was so happy. I don't know why I knew, I just did. I believed. The service was life changing to me. I don't know if everyone felt that way, but I sure did.

I was starting back to work on Tuesday. Monday was a holiday, Martin Luther King Day. We traveled through a horrible blizzard to get to Dr. Garcia's office for it. Now I'm happy I'm numb all around that area from the surgery; didn't feel a thing! God is so good!

I was starting back to work on Tuesday. One of my customers who had become a dear friend and had also been praying fervently for me sent me an email that morning and I replied:

> Jody,
> I'm actually working today. God is so good!!
> We had the healing service yesterday for me at church. Pastor Gordy Robbins at the Falconer First Baptist church did it. It was something that God had laid on my heart, so I asked him to do it. That is the church I was raised in and I know everyone on the board and all the deacons and deaconesses. We are going to start going there again and working at building a Sunday School. There is no one there under 50 and I don't want it to just end up closing in a few years.
> But the song you showed me,
> It has a few verses that God has given me through all this…
> The night that I found out I had cancer back this past summer, I was up all night crying and praying and reading my bible, but not comforted like I would have been if I wouldn't have been trying to carry all that by myself.
> He gave me 2 Kings 20:5

I have heard your prayers, I have seen your tears; surely I will heal you.

And then later that night Psm 45:1

Be still and know that I am God.

When I was doing chemo:

Psm 50:15

Call upon me in the day of trouble; I will deliver you and you will glorify me

And

Psm 40:3

He has put a new song in my mouth— praise to our God. Many will see it and fear and will trust in the Lord.

I still have some healing to do from the surgeries and then radiation, but I have felt answered prayers and God's presence throughout this whole ordeal and it has been such an incredible journey. God is good —all the time. ☺

Thank you for all your encouragement throughout my trials. ☺ I love you Jody.

Jamie

These were all the verses I spoke about at the healing service when Pastor Gordy asked if I had anything I'd like to say. He had put a new song in my mouth, and I was never going to miss an opportunity to give God the glory for my healing and for him holding me through this past year. That footprints in the sand saying really had meaning to me now. I truly felt that God had carried me through. I was forever grateful and thankful.

I was back to working; it was kicking my butt. I was only a couple weeks from major surgery, and I was still healing, but I was healing very well, and I was getting stronger each day. I was pretty much working and sleeping. But life was getting back to normal. I only had radiation and a couple more surgeries left. And the last one was just getting the mediport taken out. That'd be a while. They liked to have it in for a year to eighteen months after you complete chemo in case your cancer returns. But I was through the worst of it. I'd had the chemo and the major surgery. Actually, more like three in one. The mastectomy, the expander placed, and the reduction on the right side—so they matched.

Keith drove up to Buffalo and picked up his new sawmill on Wednesday, January 20. I was traveling out of town that day with Bobby and Abi to Wellsville for a call. Another sweet friend there. I realize how blessed I am.

That was the week that a dear friend Harold died. Harold and Delores had been the master and mistress of ceremony at our wedding. We grew up with the kids. They were family. Harold had stopped by during the summer on one last trip up from Florida to see his family and friends. He was dying of cancer. I hate cancer. It was hard to go to this. I don't think I had survivor's guilt because Harold was twenty-five years older than me, but I felt bad that he was gone. I loved him and his family. Delores had died a couple years back from Alzheimer's. I would miss them both. But they were born-again Christians and I knew I'd see them again. So many of my people were now gathered in heaven and not here anymore. I think it was especially hard because Harold's whole family had moved to Florida, and they really didn't have too much reason to come back to the area now.

My company had the Holiday Party this weekend, but I didn't go this year. I didn't have enough energy to work through the week and also do anything on the weekend. I rested. Period. But if I did rest, I could get through the week, so I was mending and getting stronger, and the worst was behind me now.

On Wednesday, January 27, Keith got his sawmill together and made his first cut with it. The weather had taken a wonderful turn for the better and it was almost fifty degrees and sunny out.

We got back to our Saturday routine with Zoie coming over at nine and me making Mickey Mouse pancakes with chocolate chips. Not very healthy, I guess, with the chocolate chips, but it'll make for great memories someday for her with her gramma!

Groundhog Day came, but who cares what that little rodent says? We've had an amazing winter so far. We could take a little more winter if we had to. February was here. I was healing and getting ready to start my radiation and get this thing over with!

We celebrated the Super Bowl with Keith's almost-famous spaghetti and the family. The family was over until half time. I think the hardest I ever heard my dad laugh was several years ago, when a Super Bowl commercial showed a couple on a romantic winter sleigh ride. The man gave his lady friend the candle to hold while he bent down to get something from the floor of the sleigh. In the meantime, the horse broke wind, and it exploded over the candle onto the girl's face and hair and charred everything. Hilarious. I don't know if it was my dad bent over laughing so hard that made it so memorable or the commercial, but I'm guessing that seeing your dad laughing so hard he's crying is the ticket. So I was addicted to watching Dad watch the Super Bowl commercials in hopes that they'd come up with another one that would make Dad laugh like that again. It's wonderful to have everyone together, and Keith's spaghetti was pretty darn good too. It felt good to eat without getting sick.

I had an infection on the right side from one of the incisions. I was on antibiotics and I was seeing Dr. Garcia this week. He said this is common but it sure scared me. It looked really mean and it popped the incision open for about an inch and just looked really scary to me.

I now had to go once a month to have my port flushed. Keith had told me never to look at the needle while I was getting chemo. I didn't then, but I accidentally did this time, not thinking about it. Holy smokes! That's one big, stinkin' needle! Yikes! I'd go once a month until they took it out to keep it open and working by having it flushed.

This month was particularly busy. I had the follow-up appointment with Dr. Garcia, a meeting with Dr. Tong (who would be in charge of my radiation), a port flush, and a CT scan. Phew!

I did have the CT scan in Olean. This is where I had my first CT scan. The only difference was that this time, I was wearing a wig. When I read all the information, it said I had to take it off. I hadn't brought anything to wear on my head, and I remembered that room being really cold, and I didn't want my bald head hanging out for anyone to see. I didn't consider myself vain, but I didn't want anyone to see me bald. I looked bad bald. They let me keep the wig on but warned that if there was anything at all metal on it, it'd end up attached to the machine during the test. I was really glad I got to keep it, and it stayed on the whole time. I know in the whole scheme of things, it's a small thing, but I was happy I didn't have to take my wig off. Now, I just needed to wait for the results.

We celebrated my fifty-ninth birthday that Friday together. Mom and Dad came up and Marcie, Michael and Zoie came over. Marcie got me a beautiful frame for Zoie's kindergarten picture and a sign for in front of it that said "Grandkids Rock." They sure do and I don't know what I'd have done without my beautiful granddaughter to help keep me laughing through all this. My mom and dad bought me a beautiful diamond bracelet. I felt happy to be alive and be here with my beautiful family celebrating another birthday. I didn't know if I'd get this one, I was feeling blessed to be here, alive to celebrate. We talked about planning a trip to Disney as soon as I was done with my radiation to celebrate being a survivor. I'd never had a bucket list, but now I wanted to do this. We'd take Marcie, Michael, and Zoie and stay at one of the nicer resorts, hopefully, the Contemporary where we stayed when Keith first got sick. That way, if I got too tired, I could just hop on the monorail and get back to the hotel. Marcie and Michael were going to look into it for me. Mom and Dad weren't really interested in going but enjoyed being a part of the planning. How exciting! I had a celebration plan! We didn't include Zoie in on our plans, just in case they didn't work out.

March started my radiation. I was fitted for a mold to position me on the treatment table in the exact same spot each time. I laid on it with my arm up above my head. It was very painful to lay that way because it was still very hard for me to get my arm up like they needed because of my surgery. I don't know if it was the lymph nodes or the mastectomy or what it was, but it didn't want to go up there. But it did; ouch.

I went every day for seven weeks. I asked for the earliest appointment and got in at 8:40 a.m. That was the earliest. I'd go in there and wait with a bunch of men who were having radiation for prostate cancer. They all had to drink a bunch of water before they went in, and they were all very antsy to get in and get the treatment and get to the men's room. They joked about it a lot. I'd go in, strip to the waist, put on a hospital robe, walk down the hall, climb onto the machine with my mold forcing my arm up. I'd been tattooed with three little blue dots; one on each side and one above my left breast. They'd line up the dots with the machine by laser lights that shone from three walls that hit my tattooed dots exactly. They'd pull the sheet under me a little this way and a little that way until they were perfect. It took a lot longer to get me oriented on the table correctly than it took to get the radiation.

The technicians would line me up and leave the room. The machine would start clicking and whirling and moving all over to get into the first position. It would lock into place and then I'd hear a buzz for about fifteen seconds. Then it'd move a little bit and I'd hear a buzz for another twenty seconds. It'd move around me to the other side and I'd hear another ten or twelve seconds of buzzing, then the lens would change but the machine would stay the same for another eight seconds. Then one final move and I'd get another couple second, and I was done. Then there'd be a couple seconds of quiet, and the door would open, and one of the technicians would help me up off the table and I'd be done.

It was a little embarrassing because one of the technicians was a young man. He was very professional and nice, but I was a private person.

I wore a hospital robe to get from the changing room to the treatment room, but then they'd pull it down to my waste for the whole treatment. I was laying there in that big room, half naked. Like I said, I've always been a private person, so this was hard for me. I kept telling myself that they were medical professionals and it didn't matter to them, but it did matter to me. I was deformed and embarrassed and really cold. I did tell them that my right boob was now the best-looking boob I'd ever owned. It made them laugh a little and I felt better. The things you can learn to get used to; it's really pretty incredible.

I honestly thought that radiation was going to be a walk in the park; an inconvenience, but nothing more really. That's what it was through March. I got through the first tweny to twenty-five days not really noticing too much except a little tiredness. I'd be pretty exhausted by the end of the day of work, but I hadn't really started getting my energy back after the chemo and surgeries. I was almost used to being tired.

By the time April got here, I was starting to get burned, and it was getting a lot harder to go in for treatment each day. I could smell myself cooking. I even started wearing turtleneck shirts because I couldn't stand the smell of myself and the thought that I was pretty much getting cooked grossed me out. Big time.

My mom has a bloodhound's nose and I kept asking her if she could smell me, but she'd say no. It was either my imagination or she was trying to make me feel better. Either way, it'd be over soon. Thank you, God.

Before the end of my radiation, I had a mammogram scheduled for April 6 with Dr. Engel and his team. They were going to be keeping close tabs on me for a while. I scheduled myself in Erie to make calls that day and had the mammogram at 1:00 p.m.

I figured I'd be in and out and on my way. I went in to have the mammogram. It was a 3–D machine. I wore the cloth robe again. Nice.

They called my name and I went in and had the right side done. I mentioned that I should get this for half price since I only had one side done. I guess that's not the way it works.

I went out to sit in the waiting room because they let you know right away that everything is fine. They called my name and I went back in. They wanted to take another picture. "Okay, don't worry, I'm sure it's nothing," I told myself. They did another one targeting the upper outside quadrant. I went back out to sit and wait again. A few minutes went by, and I spent that time praying for the peace God had given me so many times through this journey. And, of course, that it wasn't cancer. I just couldn't imagine that I had more to go through.

They called me back in, but this time, we went into another room that was filled with machines. I spoke to a technician who said they saw something they wanted to take a closer look at. They'd like to do a sonogram. The technician did a sonogram right then and saw something she didn't like.

A few minutes later, a stunningly beautiful black woman with amazing hair came in to talk to me. She was my doctor for these tests. She was so pretty and so compassionate.

Knowing my history, she wanted me to come back in a couple of days to have a biopsy done. Boy, been there, done that. Phew. My mind was reeling. But one thing I did know, I had six more radiation treatments left and then we were going to Disney to celebrate and I was not going to let this ruin that celebration.

I was going to wait until I got back to have the biopsy.

I told her I was going to Disney on the twenty-second and I'd schedule the sonogram as soon as I got back. She didn't think it was wise to wait that long, and she thought it might ruin my vacation worrying that the cancer had come back. I told her that God had healed me from the first cancer, and we were going as a family to celebrate that healing. If something more had to be done, that would be a whole different battle, and we'd gear up for that when we came back. She scheduled the biopsy right then. We'd come back from Disney on Thursday and she scheduled the biopsy for the following Tuesday. She told me if I changed my mind and wanted to come sooner just call them and they'd get me in.

I got through the radiation with the last four days being what they called a "boost." This was a concentration of radiation over a very small amount of skin. This was because the cancer had invaded my skin and they wanted to be sure they cooked any cancer that was hiding. The final day of my radiation, I cried all the way through it. I don't know why, maybe because I was exhausted from the radiation or a combination of everything or just from trying to be so brave. I couldn't help it and I was still crying when the technician came in to help me off the table. But it was the gal who came in (maybe the young man had heard me sniffling and they'd decided not to embarrass me anymore than necessary) and helped me up. I told her they were happy tears because I'd now made it through the chemo and the radiation, and the only thing in my future was a couple surgeries and I was good to go. To God be the glory!

I was almost there. I had a couple of tests coming up and then we were Disney bound! Planning the Disney trip had been such a fun thing to do. And having it be a surprise for Zoie was even more fun. It had given me something magical to look forward to, and I think that was just the ticket. We were going to Disney to introduce Zoie to Minnie and Mickey. How fun!

> I want to thank you for holding me up in prayer this past year.
> I finished my last radiation treatment on Wednesday—even got a diploma! :0) It will probably be a month before they schedule any tests to determine medically what I know already. I feel

great and I know that God has answered prayers and healed me. I am surrounded by God's favor.

I have felt so blessed and loved through this past year as you all have prayed me through this. God has been so sweet and tender and present for me through my entire journey. He not only held me and protected me, but He gave me such wonderful family, co-workers and friends to help me through it. I cannot tell you how much your support and prayers have meant to me- it was what kept me moving forward through the chemo, surgeries and finally the radiation. I couldn't have done it without each one of you. Thank you.

I hope none of you ever have to go through a big life trial, but if you ever do, please know that I will be your prayers warrior. It will be my honor to stand with you in prayer. The God who created each one of us is there, just a prayer away waiting to give you the peace that passes understanding. It's real and I've felt it several times this past year.

Next Friday my family and I will be leaving for a 5 day vacation to introduce Zoie to Mickey Mouse! (it's a surprise for her—how fun!!) I wish all of you could come with us to celebrate!

I will be forever thankful for each of you. It is no accident that we are here at this time in this place to become not just acquaintances, but friends and family. I thank God for you. I pray that He blesses you as you have blessed me.

Thank you.
With sincere love,
Jamie

Now to Him who is able to do exceedingly abundantly above all that we ask or think, according to the power that works in us, to Him be glory

Eph 3:20

Disney was magical. We stayed at the Contemporary in case I got tired. I could just jump on the monorail and get right to our room. We started off with a scooter for me because I was pretty exhausted, but I gave that up by the middle of the first day and turned it back in. I'd rather do less than bother with that thing. Besides, I'm the reason they coined the phrase *woman driver*, so it wasn't safe to give me a scooter at Disney! So Keith and I ended up sitting now and again rather than walking to a ride. Marcie, Michael, and Zoie would get us on the way back to the next ride, and we'd people watch for a bit and rest. That was fascinating too! It was all just plain magical and exactly the thing I needed to celebrate getting through the worse of my treatments. I couldn't swim because of my burns, and I had to bring some extra medical stuff to treat the radiation site but that was minor. I was alive and I was at Disney with my family and it was magical. My feet were killing me! But I was having a blast.

Each night, we watched the fireworks from our balcony on the fifth floor, eating cookies I'd stuffed into my Disney mug from one of the buffets (might be something wrong with that, now that I'm thinking about it) and I'd thank God for giving me this wonderful experience. I felt so blessed!

We got back on Thursday very late as planned. I had my biopsy on Tuesday as planned. It was fairly quick and the doctor and nurse who took care of me were so incredibly sweet. That beautiful doctor with the amazing hair sat and talked to me about Disney for about ten minutes before we went in to get the biopsy done. She had a little boy and was thinking of taking him soon, so I was telling her what we did.

The biopsy was done and I was on my way. That was Tuesday and they said they'd let me know as soon as the reports came back. I tried not to think about it. I kept praying to God to give me peace about it either way. I truly believed that he had healed me of the cancer, but I didn't know what plans he had for me, so I didn't know what I would be going through moving forward. I just knew that I was really hoping we were done. I was praying and asking everyone to pray with me.

On Friday of that week, Dr. Engel himself called me to tell me that everything was good and there was no cancer. He wanted to tell me before the weekend so I didn't have to worry about it all that time.

I cried. I called my mom and we cried. I texted Marcie and cried. I called Keith and cried. I was so stinkin' relieved. I knew God would get me through whatever I had to do, but I was really tired and I didn't want to be brave or strong or anything for a while. I just wanted to rest and heal and thank God for his amazing answered prayer for my life. Cancer didn't surprise him. He was all knowing and powerful and prepared, and he carried me through so much of this past year's journey. I was just so relieved. I felt so blessed.

Now my next procedure was swapping out the expander for the permanent implant. I went to see Dr. Garcia a couple of weeks later, and he said it'd be a while before my skin was healed enough for surgery. I saw him in May and he said he'd look at it in another month and see. I saw him in June and he said the same thing. I was going in once a month to have my port flushed to my chemotherapy doctor's office, and once a month to see if my skin had healed enough to do the last surgery. But on a brighter note, my hair was starting to look almost like I wanted it to be cut that way. My beautician had cut it around my ears and it looked like a really short hairstyle now. It was incredibly curly, and I had way more gray than before, but I had hair! Yay! I also had hair fuzz growing all over my face. What's up with that? She was also waxing my face where hair shouldn't grow on ladies. Yuck! She did that a couple of times and it quit growing. Thank goodness! So I was getting my port flushed, my skin checked, my hair shaped, and my face waxed every month. Boy, was I becoming high maintenance! But I felt like I was starting to come back to being me again.

On May 14, we celebrated my dad's eighty-fifth birthday. It was a wonderful celebration and almost all the kids and grandkids were there. There are several pictures of me with that really short haircut. It's not horrible; which is good, because everyone has copies of them.

On May 21, we celebrated Zoie's seventh Annual Tea Party. We started that tradition when Zoie was five months old, and we've continued it each year since. So this year was the seventh annual. It was especially sweet too because Joy was able to be here for it this year with her daughter Heidi. It was very special to me to have them here for it.

June came and I still wasn't ready for the surgery. I had my port flushed. Life was starting to get back to normal. I wasn't scheduling all my calls around a doctor's appointment. I only had those two in June. Life was good.

Keith and I celebrated our forty-first wedding anniversary. Another reason to be thankful; another day to mark my victory over cancer.

The weather had turned very hot. It was a beautiful summer. Dad had started his garden and it was looking good. He'd work in it for a bit and go sit for a while to cool off. It was a struggle for him to do it, but he loved his gardens and working on them. He had the place flowered up like he said he was going to do when he first moved in. He'd come up every day and tell me about what he'd ordered from his seed catalog and where he was going to plant them and what beds he was going to start. The place was looking good. He'd also comment on how wonderful it was that God had healed me. "You're going to be just fine, Jamie," he'd tell me. "I'm not, but you are." I'd say, "Then let's pray for ten years for you and thirty for me," and smile. I really enjoyed having Dad and Mom here and so did Keith. It sure had been a blessing while I was getting through all the treatments. Only one big surgery and one small surgery left. I was almost there. Thank you, God.

On June 30, Mom called me downstairs to see Dad. Something was wrong. I got down there and he was laying on his bed, and I sat beside him and asked what was going on. He was having terrible pain everywhere from his waist up. After talking for a minute, I told him I thought he was having a heart attack. I told him we could drive him to the hospital in about three minutes or we could call the ambulance. He said it's too much talking, just do something. That's so like Dad. He insisted on walking to the car. Keith had come downstairs to help, so we walked beside him to get him to the car. It was the longest three-minute car ride I've ever taken.

We got him to the hospital and they took him right in and checked him out and told us that he was in fact having a heart attack, and they were going to star flight him to Erie for a procedure to open up the arteries. His heart wasn't getting the blood it needed and there was blockage. Not a huge deal, but a shock, considering we never knew he had any heart issues. He'd gone through yearly physicals and had EKGs and never once had they mentioned that he had any heart issues. This explained the "weak spells" he had. All this time, we'd blamed them on his cancer medicine. Wow. It was two in the morning, and Mom and I were driving to Erie and Janet was coming out early in the morning.

They did testing on Dad first thing in the morning. Janet, Mom, and I waited for the results. We thought they'd probably put the stints in while they did the testing, and he'd be right as rain and home in a day.

The doctor came to us in the waiting room and said he needed by-pass surgery to save his life. There was too much damage and block-age to do anything else. This was not at all what we were expecting.

I felt we should do it—probably because I didn't want to lose Dad. But he was so strong and had so much life left in him. Janet, always the strong, practical one, thought it was selfish to put an eighty-five year old man through open-heart surgery. It was awful to think of him trying to recover from that at his age. Mom's thoughts were that Dad never wanted to do anything special to prolong his life. Do we strengthen up his heart so he dies a painful death from bone cancer—don't forget that. We all loved Dad with all our hearts, but we didn't know what to do. We held hands and I prayed, standing there in the surgery waiting room of the hospital. "We don't know what to do, God. Please show us your way and help us do what your will is and what is best for Dad. We know you love him even more than we even know how to love, so your will be done. Guide us Lord. Amen." And we walked up to his room to meet him.

The heart doctor assigned to him came up to talk to us. He was a wonderful man, brutally honest, but wonderful. He said most of Dad's heart was blocked and the rest of it was dead. The pain from that part of the heart dying was over now, and this heart attack didn't kill him, but the next one would. He needed bypass, but there wasn't a surgeon that would operate on him. He was eighty-five, had can-cer, and had this much damage to his heart. There was nothing they could do but try to get him as strong as they could with medicine and send him home. This was our answer. God has shown us what to do. We asked for guidance and it didn't get any clearer than this.

Steven, my brother, and his wife Jill, got there then. Not the news we wanted to hear, but we clung to the "bring him home" part. We just wanted to get him home.

We did get him home on the fourth of July 2016. We didn't have a clue what we were in for. Janet did. She'd worked in nursing homes first as an aide when she was young and now as the billing coordinator for the local one. She knew, but Mom and I were determined to let him have a beautiful summer sitting outside looking at his gardens. Me, with only one arm of any use because of my surgeries, and Mom, a seventy-nine-year-old woman. She was amazingly healthy, but still seventy-nine. We were going to be his nurse maids. We tried. It was actually almost comical. Dad maintained his sense of humor and laughed at our feeble attempts. He got so weak he could barely breathe. I took vacation days and Janet took vacation days, and by Friday even Mom and I said, Okay, we couldn't physically do it. Janet said we needed to call hospice and get respite. It was a break to let the family rest. She called but said we'd better eat our Wheaties because nothing ever happens on Friday. We'd have to make it until Monday and then they'd put him in a hospice section of the hospital and we could sleep at night. So again, we took Dad's hand and we all held hands around him and prayed. "God, we are at that point again that we don't know what's best to do. Please guide us and show us your way. We love you and we know you love us. Thank you for the love and hope you give us. Bless Dad. Bless Mom. Amen." Just before we were done praying, the phone rang. It was hospice. Dad's doctor was out of the country and the hospice doctor had approved the respite and the ambulance was coming at 4:00 pm to pick Dad up. Even Janet cried at that immediate, obvious answer to our prayers. God is so gentle and loving.

Keith wrote this on Facebook for Dad:

> Over a week ago my father-in-law had a heart attack. A weaker man would have died from it, but Jim was strong. Even though we were to find out later that his heart was a mess and had been for a long time, we never knew he had any heart troubles. We blamed all his weakness on cancer.
>
> He'd spent the day planting and hauling dirt and digging. Things he loved and was good

at. That evening Jackie called us and said to come down, something was terribly wrong. Several tests and a star flight to Hamot later, we were told there was nothing they could do for him but they would try to make his heart stronger with medicine.

We brought him home on July 4th and the girls, Jackie, Janet and Jamie all cared for him round the clock. He used my oxygen until they could get him some of his own. It took a grueling trip to the doctor to get his own oxygen approved. But God was in all of this. The trip to the doctor changed his care from Home health care to Hospice and that is when things started changing; just in time.

He was getting progressively weaker each day and it was getting harder and harder for the girls to help him as much as he needed. By Friday Hospice brought him to WCA by ambulance and he has been resting in Hospice respite care. What a wonderful organization that is. This has given the girls time to sleep. They have still spent each day with him round the clock. He has become unresponsive for the most part and his body is starting to shut down. He told Janet on Friday when she left that he hoped he didn't see her the next day; he was ready to see what was on the other side.

This time since the heart attack has been very rough on everyone and it's very difficult to witness, but I think it's given everyone time to say goodbye and time to accept that life is going to go on shortly without Jim. And after watching him lay in bed like this, everyone knows that heaven is by far the best option. It's difficult, but knowing that he is saved and headed for heaven is a comforting fact. Even though we will all miss him more than we realize now we have had time to accept his passing. We don't like it, but we can accept it. He is going to leave a huge hole in the family, but it's a strong family. It has troubles just like every other family, but there has been a lot of love and Jim was there in the center of it all with Jackie.

They've been married for 62 years this past March—65 years if you count when they started dating. That's a wonderful lifetime of love.

We are waiting for the phone call to let us know that this good man's life here on earth has come to an end and his time in heaven has begun.

Here's to a life well lived.

God was so amazing. He'd paved the way ahead of our needs and now was holding us, even carrying us, through this hard time. Dad went to the hospital on Friday, July 8. We'd have five days and then they'd take him in Janet's nursing home. That, too, was an answered prayer. They'd found room for him. I'm sure it was because Janet had worked there and my dad had even worked there as a courier for them, but I also believe God had a hand in it. They can't kick people out to make room!

Tuesday was his last day of respite. Mom was talking to the nurse about keeping him at the hospital in respite a couple more days and what the fee would be per day. My daughter Marcie said Dad must have heard that and decided he didn't want Mom to pay any more money to have him hang around, so he died that day—the last day of respite. Mom and Janet and I gathered around Dad in his hospital bed. He was already gone and in heaven, but we prayed to God. We thanked him for Dad, such a wonderful husband, father, and man. We praised God for giving him to us for eighty-five years and we thanked him for his life and how Dad had blessed each of our lives. When we were done, we saw that the nurse had been in the room waiting for us to finish. She told us she was moved by our faith. Praise God.

We buried Dad on the July 15. He had full military honors and it was so moving. The vets came and did Taps and the twenty-one gun salute. Beautiful.

I wrote this for his funeral.

> To a life well lived.
>
> Dad was always a man of great character and integrity. He came from very humble beginnings and joined the Navy at 17. He came home to marry the love of his life, Mom. They started their beautiful 62 year love story and made a wonderful life for themselves and us three kids. I have such wonderful memories of my childhood surrounded by family and friends and laughter; always lots of laughter. Our home seemed to be the gathering place for friends and family to celebrate any occasion with a get together. It was a magical childhood and always at the center of it were Mom and Dad and the love they shared for each other and us.
>
> Mom was always a sweet Christian woman who taught us to love the Lord and follow His teachings. My Dad always supported that belief but he didn't share it until years (and hundreds of hours of prayer) later when he walked the aisle on Easter Sunday to the alter and accepted Jesus Christ as his Lord and Savior. What an awesome prayer answering God we serve.
>
> Dad retired a bit early because of a cancer diagnosis but was in remission for almost 20 years. When the cancer did come back he faced it with dignity and calm. When I was diagnosed last year, he'd walk up those stairs every day that I couldn't walk down them to visit with me and tell me I was going to get better. I'm so grateful he got to see that. God's timing is perfect.

We didn't know Dad had a bad heart. Any weakness he had we blamed on the cancer or his medicine. We weren't really prepared to lose him so quickly, but God's timing is perfect even in Dad's death. After his heart attack we saw God's hand in so many things that happened. He was there with us opening doors and paving the way. We prayed so many times for His help and guidance and we'd see Him working almost before we finished the prayer. He provided for Dad and for us each step of the way. God does provide a peace that passes understanding if we just trust Him and lean into him during the hard times. I felt it during my treatments and we felt it during the two weeks we cared for Dad. You can certainly see it through the strength God has given Mom to walk through this valley. What a faithful, loving God we serve.

This good man's life here on earth has come to an end and his time in heaven has begun. I'm sure it's a grand reunion there. So many people have passed over and will be waiting for him. But first he will see his savior Jesus face to face and I know he'll hear those words, "Well done my good and faithful servant". And then I think God will bring him to His garden . . . with no weeds. I think that will be heavenly for Jim Hopkins.

There is a huge hole left by Dad's death. Our hearts are forever scarred. But having a Dad you love enough to leave a scar is a blessing. You were loved and will be greatly missed Dad. I guess we'll fill that hole up with those beautiful memories you left us with.

Here's to a life well lived.

My final big surgery, the one where we swap out the expander for the implant, was finally scheduled for August 4. I arrived at the hospital at 5:30 a.m. with Keith and Marcie. My surgery was scheduled for 7:30 am. The hospital is beautiful and overlooks Lake Erie. The waiting room for Keith and Marcie had a gorgeous view of the water.

Dr. Garcia was so sweet. He held my hand while they were getting me ready in the operating room. The nurse asks me what they're going to do for me today. I responded, "You're gonna give me the cutest boobs in Jamestown." They all laughed.

I was out of surgery without complications and on my way home by 2:00 p.m. I was also on vacation for the next week. I probably wasn't going to feel like vacation, but I have a week to recover. I went back on Monday a week and a half later to get my stitches out, and I had an infection. I got antibiotics for the infection. I guess it's very common with radiated skin that won't heal well. I had a follow up visit with Dr. Engel, the cancer surgeon, that Wednesday and a port flush on Friday. And then I went weeks without a doctor's appointment! Nobody knows how wonderful that feels if you haven't been really sick. I'm thankful for each doctor that cared for me. I pray daily for them, but I'm really tired of trying to live around all the appointments. It felt so freeing not to have any doctor's appointments for weeks!

But my infection didn't go away easily. Finally, after three more appointments in September, the infection was gone. Thank you, God.

I had a three-month follow-up appointment with my oncologist in October and my monthly port flush. The doctor liked to keep the port in for twelve to eighteen months after a patient is cancer free before he'd take it out. Cancer is most likely to come back right away and that way you still have the port in. My three-month follow-up was great. All my blood work was good. Dr. Ibabao scheduled a PET scan for November 2. That would tell us what we need to know.

I had a follow-up appointment on Monday, November 7, to get the results of my PET scan. Dr. Ibabao asked me what I was there for.

I told him to know that I was cancer free and that God had healed me.

He handed me the paper with the results on it and said, "Today we celebrate a miracle. I did not expect this for you. You are cancer free."

I cried. I told him they were happy tears. I knew that God could heal me and I believed that he had. I also knew that if that wasn't what he wanted for me, He would be with me no matter what I had to go through. I was just so relieved that he and I were on the same page with what we wanted for me! I was so relieved. I was so exhausted and now I could rest and get better and put this behind me. Thank you, Lord, for this amazing miracle and this answer to all the prayers my friends and family had prayed for me.

> Hi,
>
> Today I was humbled by how much God loves me and how faithful He has been through my almost 18 month journey through cancer;

through the chemo, the surgeries and the radiation. Today I got the results of my PET scan and I am cancer free. I thank you Lord for so many answered prayers to get here. Even my doctor said this is a day to celebrate a miracle. I am.

I thank Him for giving me healing and I also thank Him for giving me such wonderful praying family and friends. I am blessed and humbled. Thank you to each one of you who lifted me up to God in prayer. You are a part of a miracle!

God has been with me the entire time, giving me the strength I've needed. Each one of you were a part of that strength and I cannot express to you how much your prayers and thoughts and cards have meant to me. I am forever grateful to each of you. Thank you from the bottom of my heart.

If you ever need someone to stand with you in prayer, I will be there to bring your name to God and He will be there for you too. It doesn't have to be a sickness. He will be there for whatever is troubling you. He loves you and so do I.

Thank you. Thank you. Thank you.

Jamie

"Now to Him who is able to do exceedingly abundantly above all that we ask or think according to the POWER that works in us, to Him be glory in the church by Christ Jesus to all generations forever and ever." (Eph. 3:20).

On Friday, November 11, I got an infection back. It was pretty bad this time. It opened up the scar of the surgery and was hot and red and swollen. I went back on antibiotics again. We fought infections on and off until Dr. Garcia finally said we might need to take everything back out and give my body a chance to rest and heal. Later, we would give it all another try from scratch.

Oh, my gosh! I didn't have it in me to do that. The battle had been too long and I was shot. I couldn't even think of having another surgery. So I asked him to give me a week. I hadn't gotten any of my prayer warriors involved in this because I thought it was just an infection. I didn't think I needed to bother God with this. I knew I needed him for the cancer, but this was nothing, or so I thought. A little antibiotic and everything was going to be fine. But that wasn't the case. I went home and called all my fervent prayer warriors and asked them to pray specifically for this infection to heal. Dr. Garcia said he'd pray with us. I went back the following week and the doctor was amazed at how much healing had gone on in one week. God is merciful and amazing and prayer is so powerful. Thank you, Lord, for the miracle of my healing.

"Not only that, but we also glory in tribulations, knowing that tribulation produces perseverance; and perseverance, character; and character, hope." (Romans 5:3–4).

December came. I had so much to be thankful for. This was our first Christmas without Dad and it was going to be hard, but it was also a cause for celebration because I was alive to celebrate. Isn't that just like life? There is never a perfect time. There is always something to worry about and someone who is sick or someone who just passed, but there is always a new baby born and someone getting better or a beautiful day that is a gift from God. I choose to take time each morning to thank God for this day and find something to be happy about in it and to celebrate. I have added a word to 1 Corinthians 4:13: "I *do* believe that I can do all things through Christ who strengthens me." He has proven that to me. And when I couldn't do it, God carried me. The footprints in the sand have new meaning to me now because God did carry me. I was too tired and weak and he carried me to this point where I can stand again in my own strength. But I knew he was right there in case I get tired again. But now I ask him each day to, "Search me oh Lord and know my heart; test me and know my anxious thoughts. See if there is any wicked way in me and lead me in the way ever lasting." (Psalm 139:23–24).

I sent out my Christmas letter:

Christmas 2016—This Christmas we are celebrating a miracle.

Unspeakable joy. That's the feeling I got not too long ago when my oncologist used the word "miracle" when he told me my test showed I was cancer free. Although my doctor is a Christian, he doesn't use that word lightly or often. To each of you who believe in the amazing power of prayer and lifted my name up to God for healing, thank you! You are a part of this incredible answered prayer we are celebrating. You have a part in this miracle! It is one of the times that God has come near this past year. And there have been several.

By human standards, this past year and a half has been a tough time, but by a different standard, it has been a time of an amazing journey where God came near. We witnessed His love and experienced His peace. Looking from that perspective now, with that journey in the rear view mirror, I can say that it was worth it just to experience God's amazing peace; the peace that passes understanding. I believe it's just a tiny sliver of how amazing heaven will one day be.

As a family, we suffered an incredible loss when Dad died. But even during those 12 days Dad was leaving this life to go start his new eternity in heaven, we saw the hand of God making everything easier for all of us as we cared for Dad those last days. We knew we weren't alone. God was holding us.

Now as Mom learns to navigate this world without Dad, it is so apparent God is giving her the help she is asking for each day. She's an amazing woman, but she'll tell you she's not strong. Her strength is in the Lord. What a beautiful testimony she lives out each day.

I think the word for 2016 was HOPE. There is incredible power in prayer and amazing hope when you are walking with God. No matter what you are going through, He is right there holding you if you'll only let Him.

From our house to yours this Christmas season, we wish you the Hope that only God can give. The Hope that was born in a stable that first Christmas Day; the Hope that comes from asking Jesus into your life as Lord and knowing that He's got you no matter what life calls you to go through. Take time this year to draw near to God who loved us enough to send his Son Jesus all those many years ago.

May you come to understand the true meaning of Christmas this year and if you already know it, may you rest in that hope this holiday season.

We love you—Merry Christmas.

Keith and Jamie

On March 20, I had my mediport taken out. It might not seem like too big of a deal. It certainly wasn't a difficult surgery. They don't even put you out for it. Thank goodness because I'd asked them to just give me a piece of rawhide to bite down on and not put me out. I got dumber and dumber after each surgery. It took me longer and longer to feel somewhat normal each time. But they didn't put you under for it. It wasn't a big surgery, but it marked the end of this journey. I'd come full circle.

Hi everyone,

This afternoon I go in to have my "port" taken out. This is my final surgery. It's just a little one, but it signals the end of my cancer journey. A new beginning. What a perfect day to have it done; the first day of Spring.

I just wanted to take a minute to thank each one of you for your prayers. I am now a walking testimony to the power of those prayers and to a loving God who is still in control and still performs miracles. You all have been a huge part of that miracle and I thank God in my prayers for each of you. I pray that God will bless you with health and happiness, but know that I will stand in prayer with any of you should you ever need it.

God lined my path with beautiful people. I thank God for allowing my path to cross with each one of yours. To God be the glory for my renewed health and each one of you He has given to me. I have learned so many lessons on this journey. One of those lessons is that God is in control and I don't have to worry. No matter what, He's got me and he's already provided a way for me through whatever life will call me to go through. So now what Jim writes on all his messages means even more to me . . . onward and most definitely, upward :0)

I love you, thank you.

Jamie

What a journey this has been. I am now a year and a half cancer free. I still have many things I'm waiting to get better. Maybe they will, maybe they won't. It doesn't really matter. They are just small things I'm learning to live with. Whether they get better or not, I have so much to be thankful for. Life, for one thing. Just waking up each day has a new joy to me. I'm alive and if I'm here, God has something he's going to teach me, or something I have learned during my journey to help someone else see God's power and love.

I still thank God each morning for the day. It doesn't matter what the weather is—and I live in western New York—so we get it all. I thank him because to me, every day is beautiful. It's not perfect, but it is beautiful. I try to be positive and hopeful always. It's not always easy, but I try and God gives me the strength to succeed most times.

I have had many opportunities to encourage women who have just found out they have cancer. My prayer list is getting longer and longer, but I remain hopeful that we'll find a cure before too much longer.

As of today, I am still cancer free. One more appointment and I get to go six months in between appointments with my oncologist. Everything is starting to fade into history, but I don't want to ever lose the thankfulness I feel for God holding me through this journey. I don't ever want to lose the hopefulness I feel at the dawn of each day. I don't know why he chose to heal me and not some other beautiful people I've known who lost their battle with cancer, but he did, so I'm always ready with a reason for the hope I feel. That hope is Jesus.

About the Author

Jamie Richir lives in New York with her husband, Keith, on a piece of land big enough for him to justify (in his mind) a backhoe and a tractor. They enjoy every square inch of their land, from the ponds and gardens in the summer, to the sugar shack up on the hill in the early spring, making maple syrup. Her whole family lives nearby. Her daughter, Marcie, with her husband, Michael, live next door in a country kind of way with her amazing granddaughter, Zoie. She enjoys being able to spend time with Jackie (her mom), Marcie, and Zoie. They have grand adventures together, even if it's just painting their nails out on the back deck. She is the North American division sales manager for **Logistics Plus**, the company that was so good to her while she was sick.